Mistaken

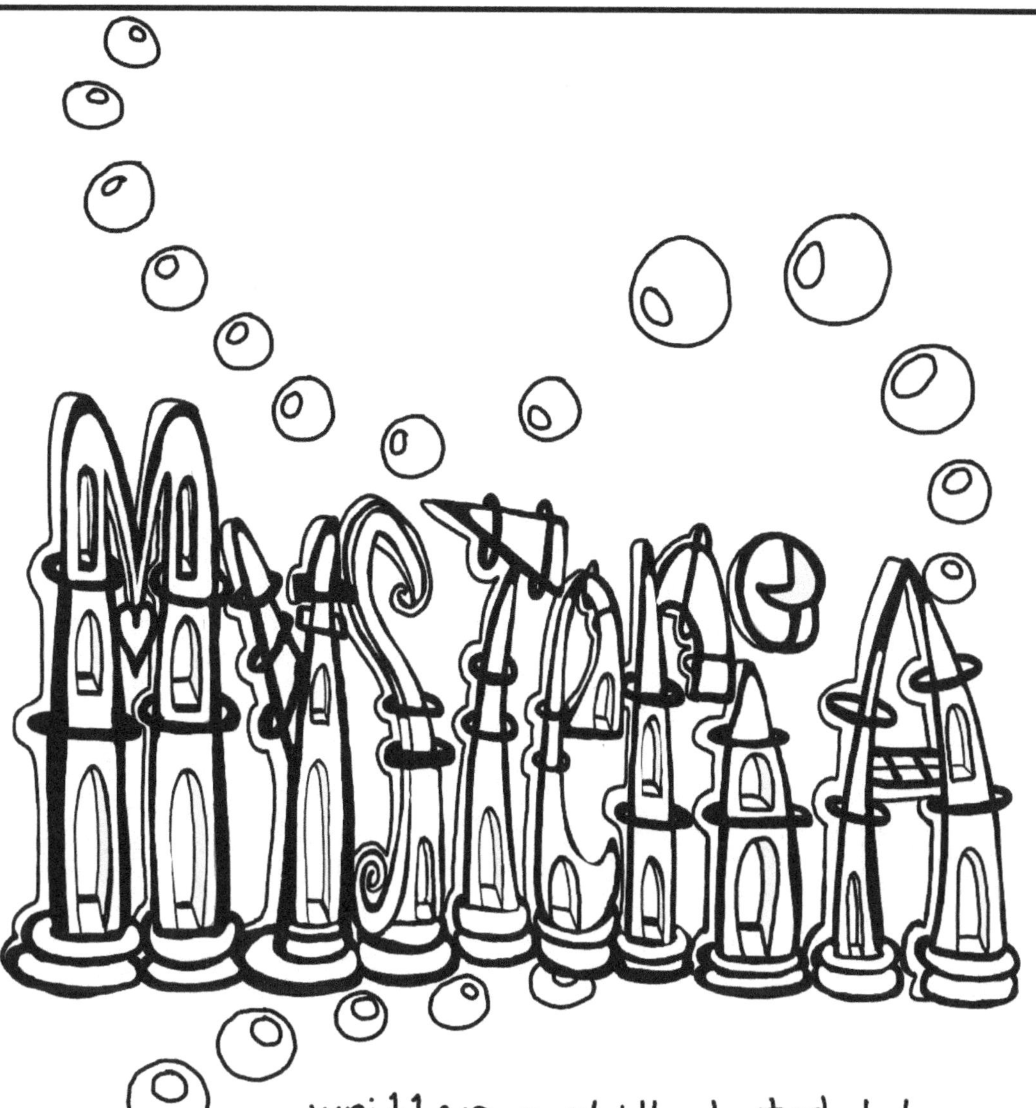

written and illustrated by:

Deborah L. McDonald

Colored by:

D.McDonald's

Mysteria

Thank you

Susan Curry

And

Christine Aldridge

For being

the driving forces getting

this book into publication.

d.mcdonald 2016

D.McDonald's

Mysteria

More of the work of D.McDonald can be found at:

www.facebook.com/DMcDonaldDesigns

Welcome to D.McDonald's
Mysteria

Many years ago a good friend suggested that I write books for children. As a life long writer and a person with a degree in secondary education, broad field English literature I laughed. "Children's books, really?" was my first response. Then I thought on it and I knew I would create a book that seemed as though it would be for a child, but not really, and Mysteria was born.

Mysteria, a place where the "haves" have what they have and the "have nots" just don't want any. A place where nothing is as it seems with strange whimsical buildings and a stranger way of life and yet once you think about it all, it does make sense or some thing no matter what will never make sense.

I consider this to be what I call an heirloom book. I strongly suggest that you take this book apart and have the pages copied on bright white card stock. Have multiple copies made and color them yourself or even better pass out copies to your family and friends to color with each person signing their pages. Then, put them all back together and have the colored pages copied onto glossy white cardstock. There are places that will spiral bind them together creating a book at no great cost. You will now have a beautiful book to pass on to generations!

There are 26 Mysterian alphabet letters in this book. This gives you the ability to spell out names or words and place them into frames and hang on a wall. Mysteria does not have any repeating letters so no copying would be involved if you choose to spell out the title and frame each letter and then also frame favorite designs which you can hang around the title creating a large wall of unique and one of a kind art!

Thank for purchasing Mysteria. Designs from my other books are included so you can sample them to see if you would like to invest in another D. McDonald publication available only on Amazon. Enjoy your coloring journey!

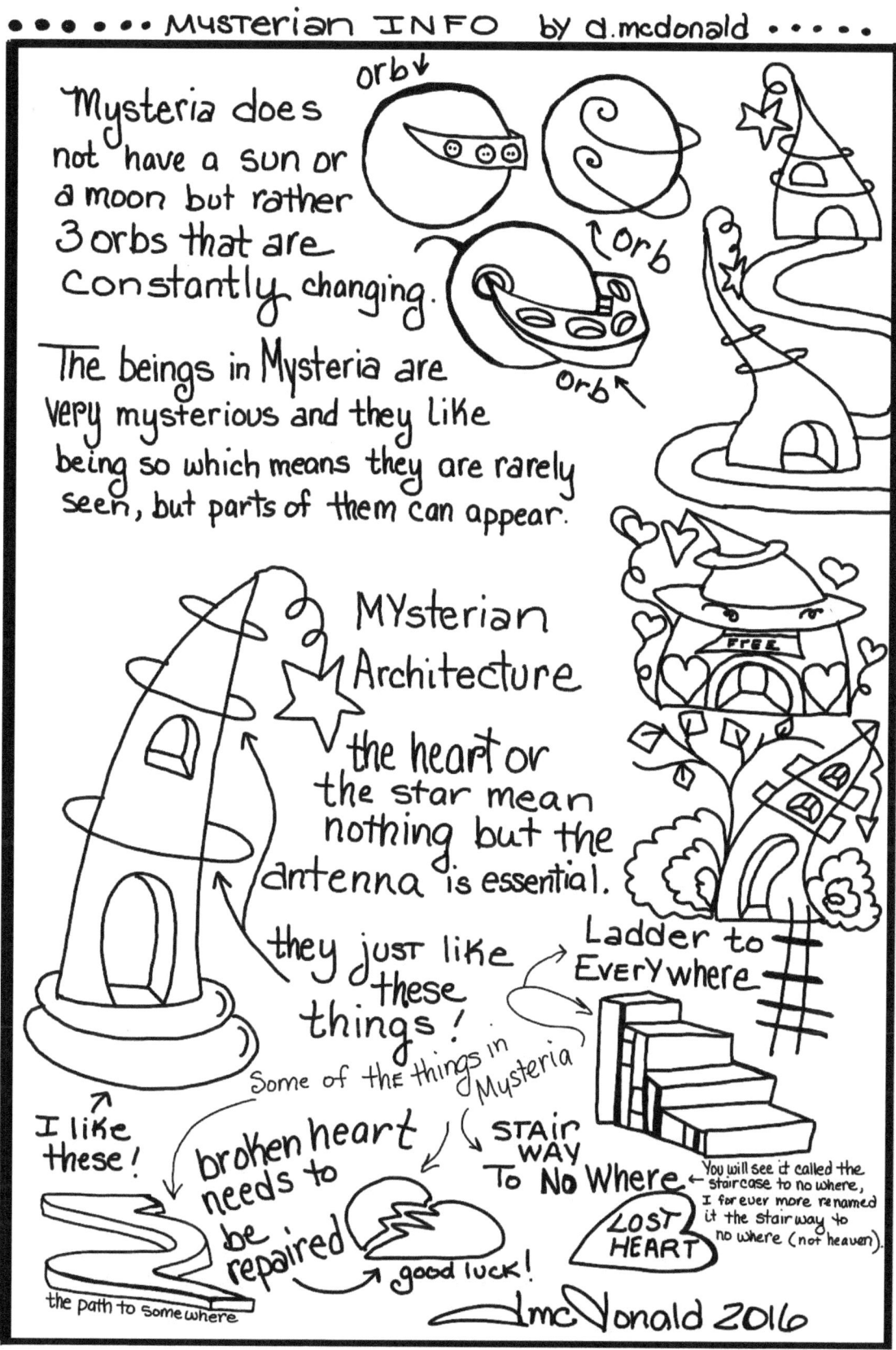

Mysteria does not have a sun or a moon but rather 3 orbs that are constantly changing.

The beings in Mysteria are very mysterious and they like being so which means they are rarely seen, but parts of them can appear.

orb↓

↑ orb

orb ↗

MYsterian Architecture

the heart or the star mean nothing but the antenna is essential.

they just like these things!

Some of the things in Mysteria

Ladder to Everywhere

FreE

I like these!

the path to somewhere

broken heart needs to be repaired

good luck!

STAIR WAY To No Where ←

You will see it called the staircase to no where, I forever more renamed it the stairway to no where (not heaven).

LOST HEART

mcDonald 2016

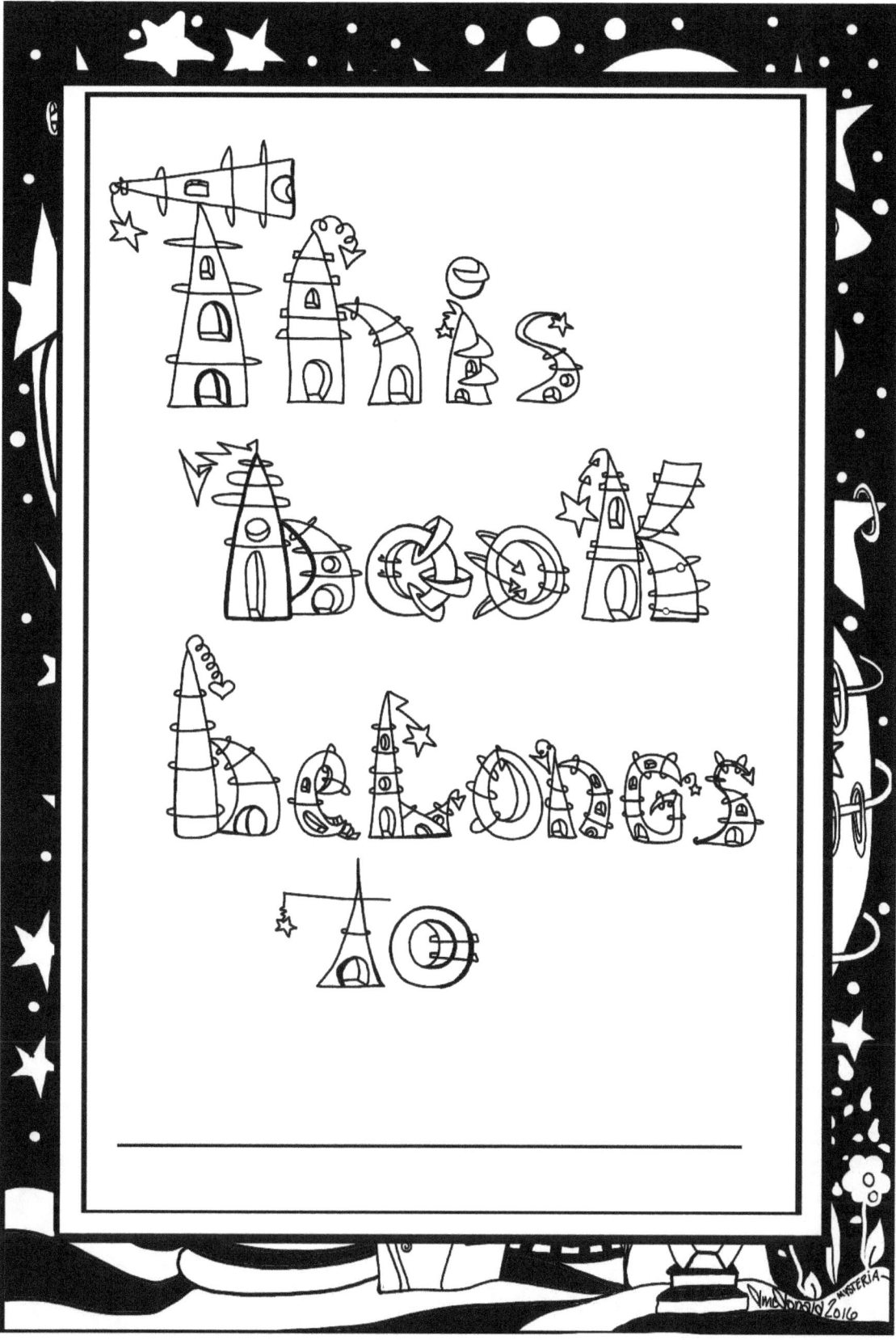

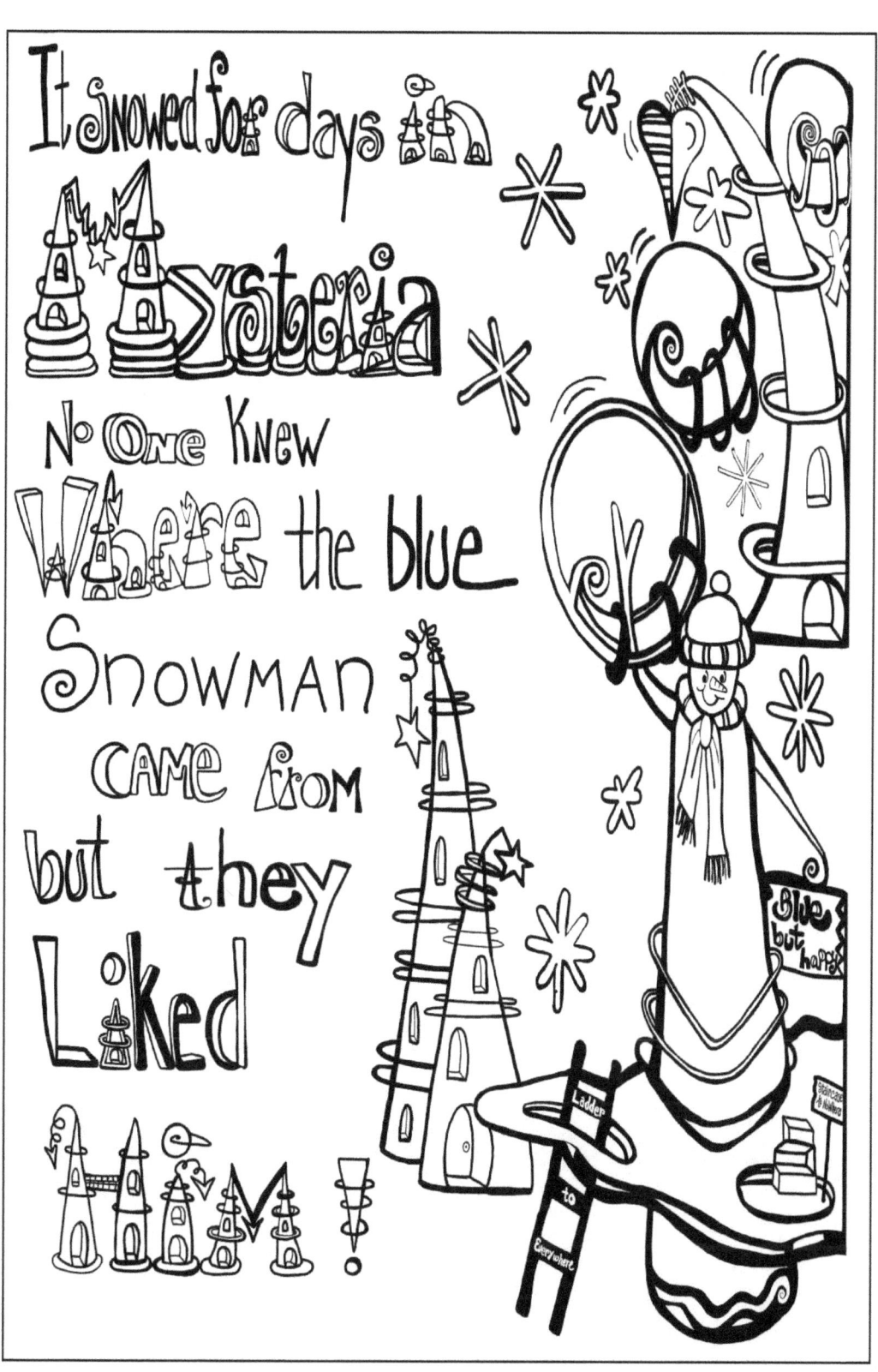

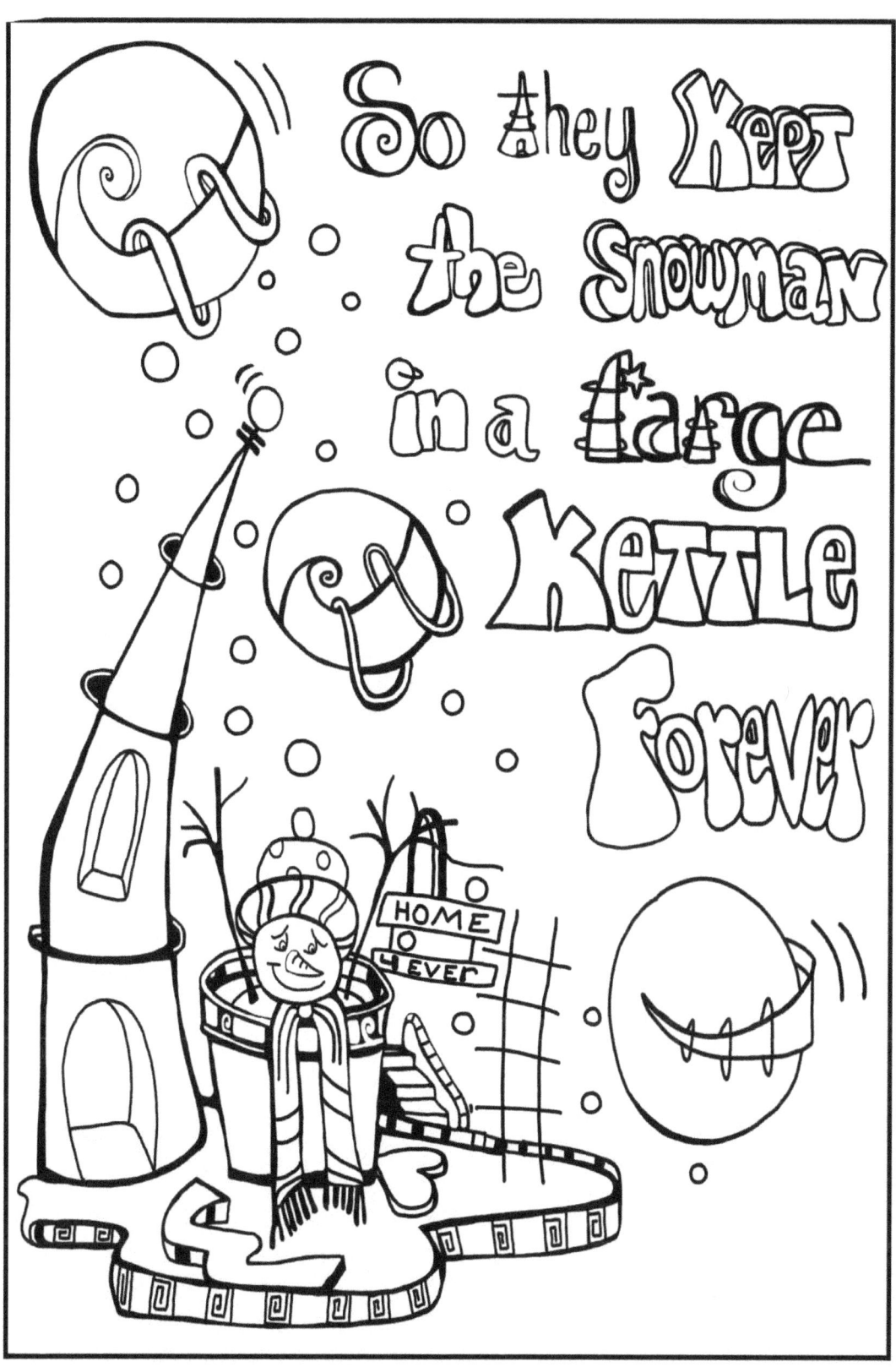

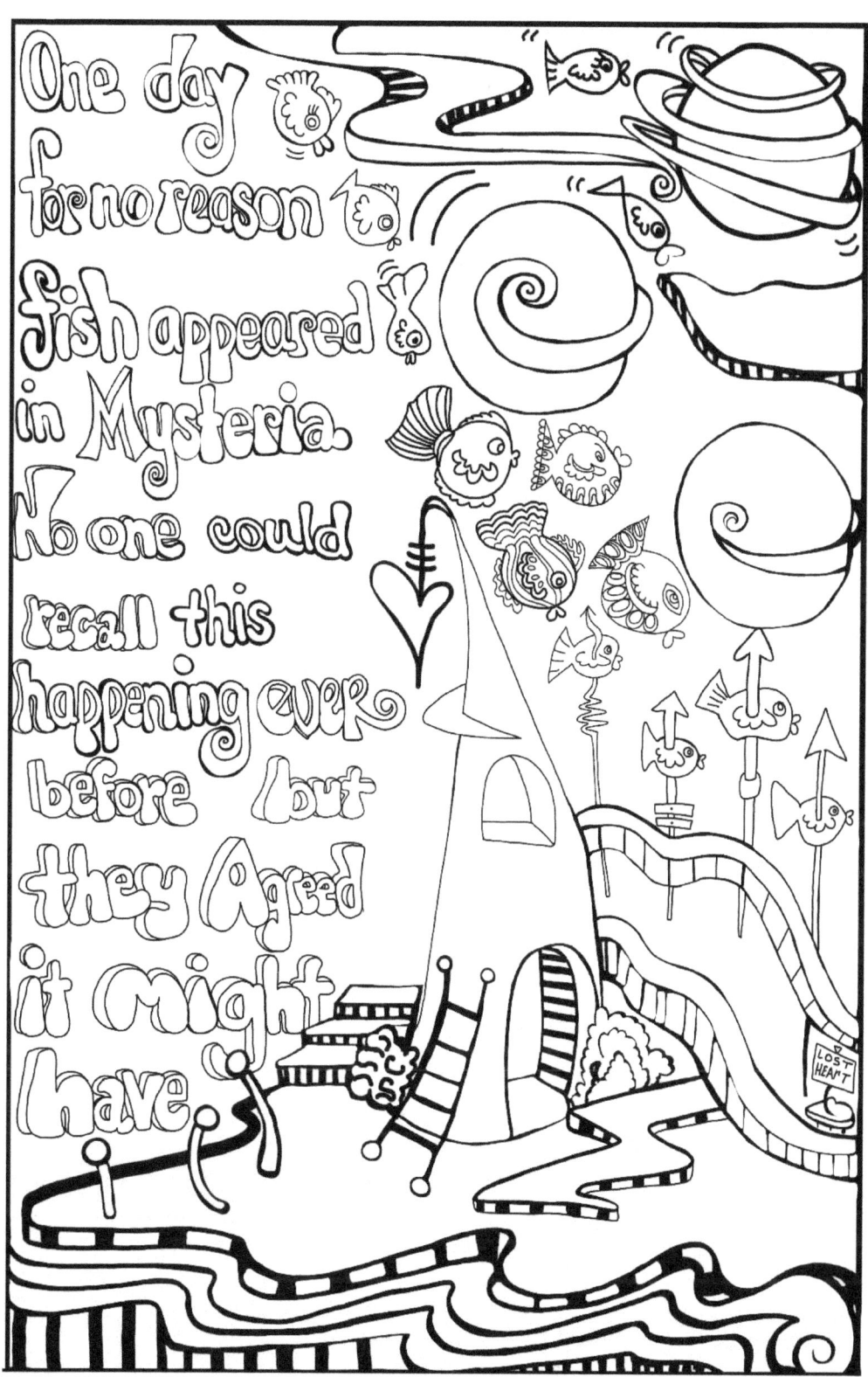

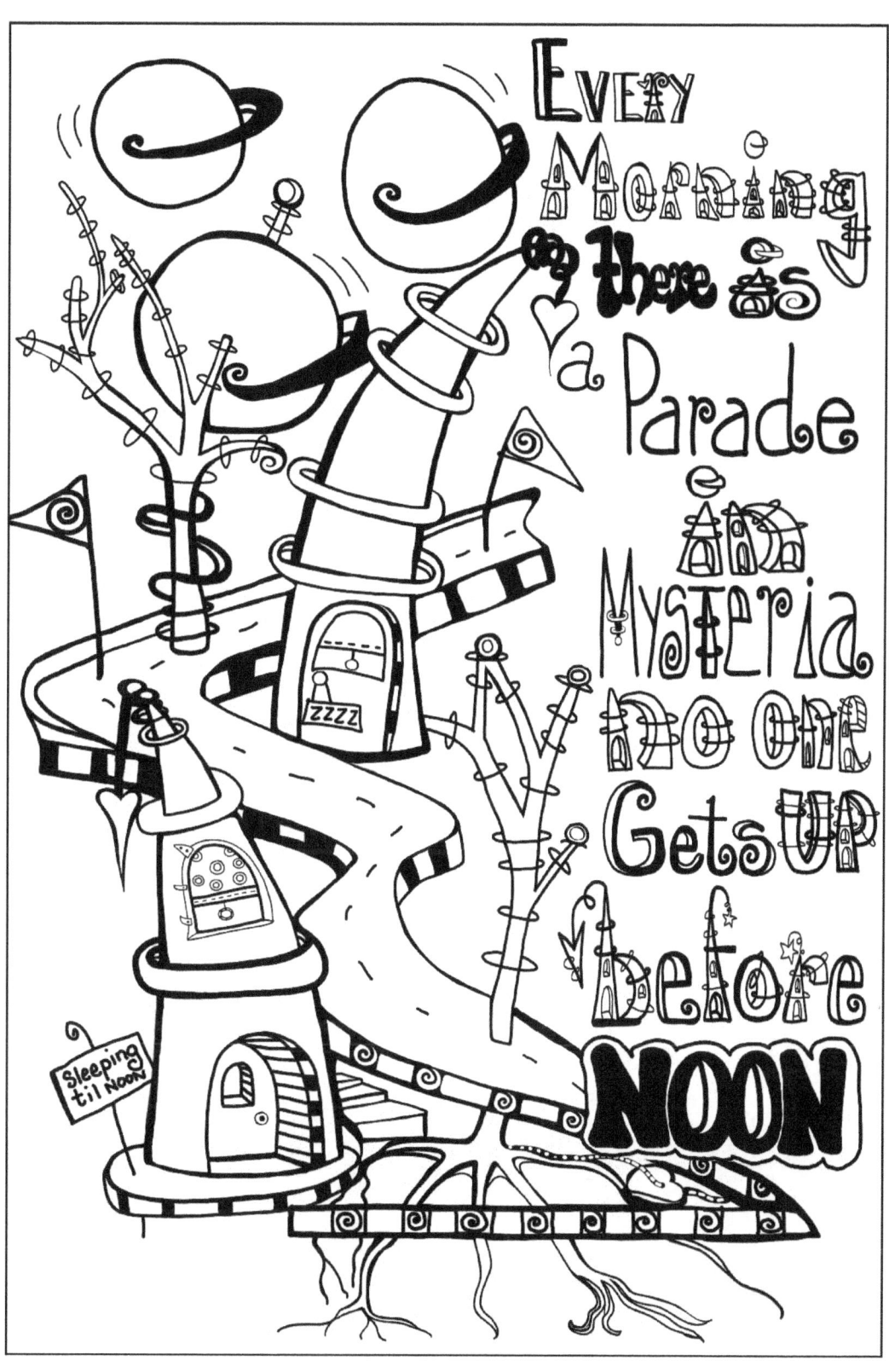

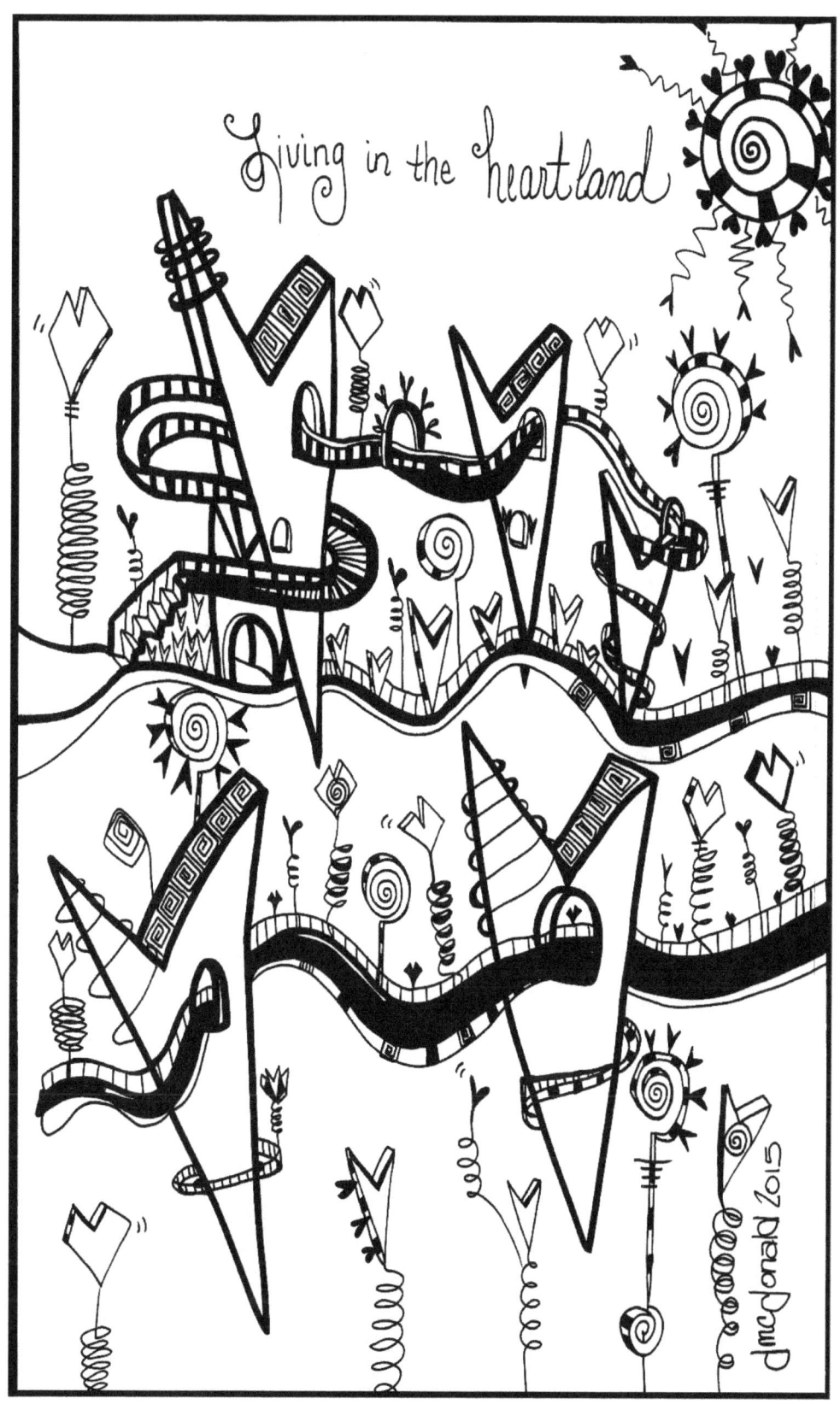

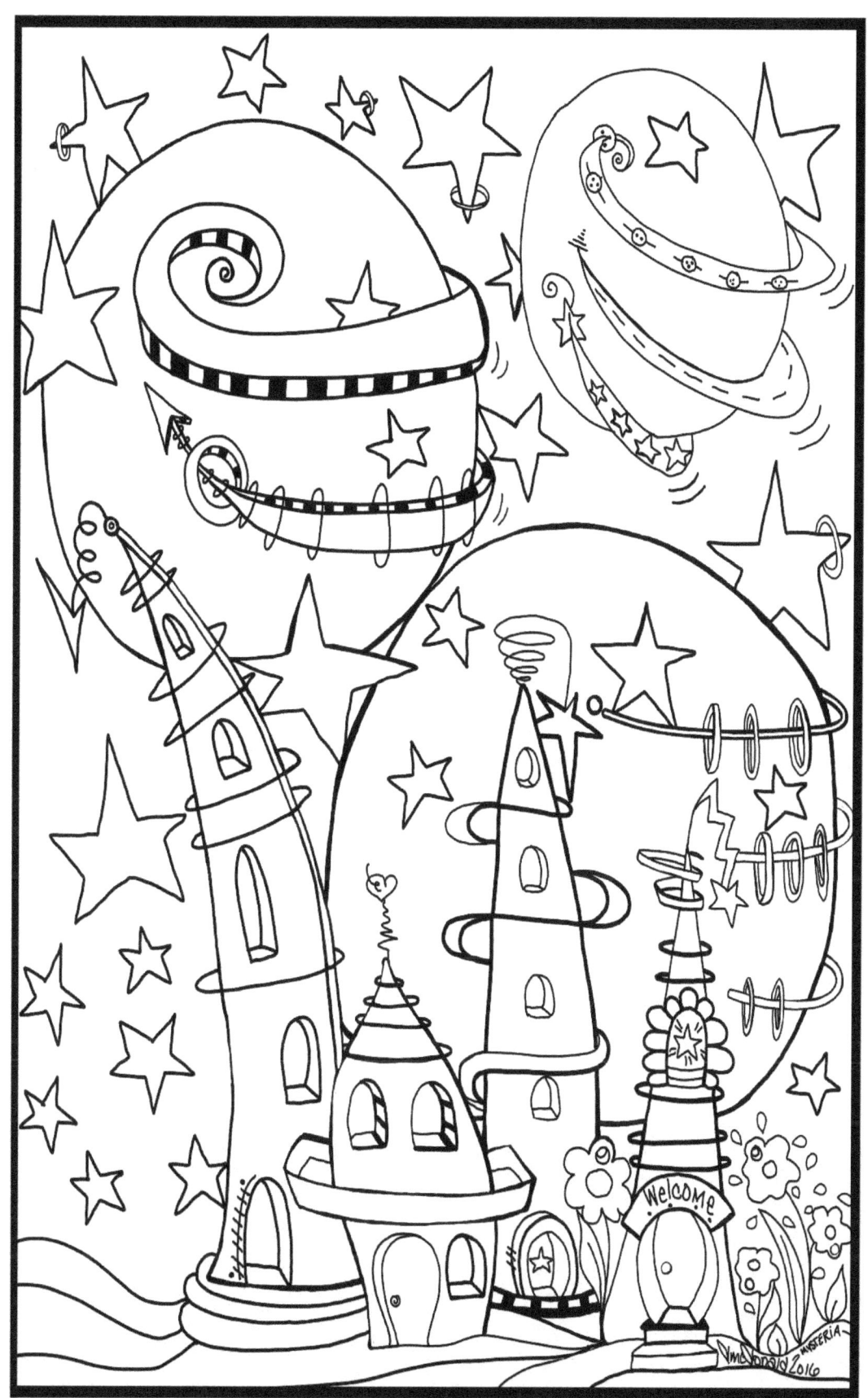

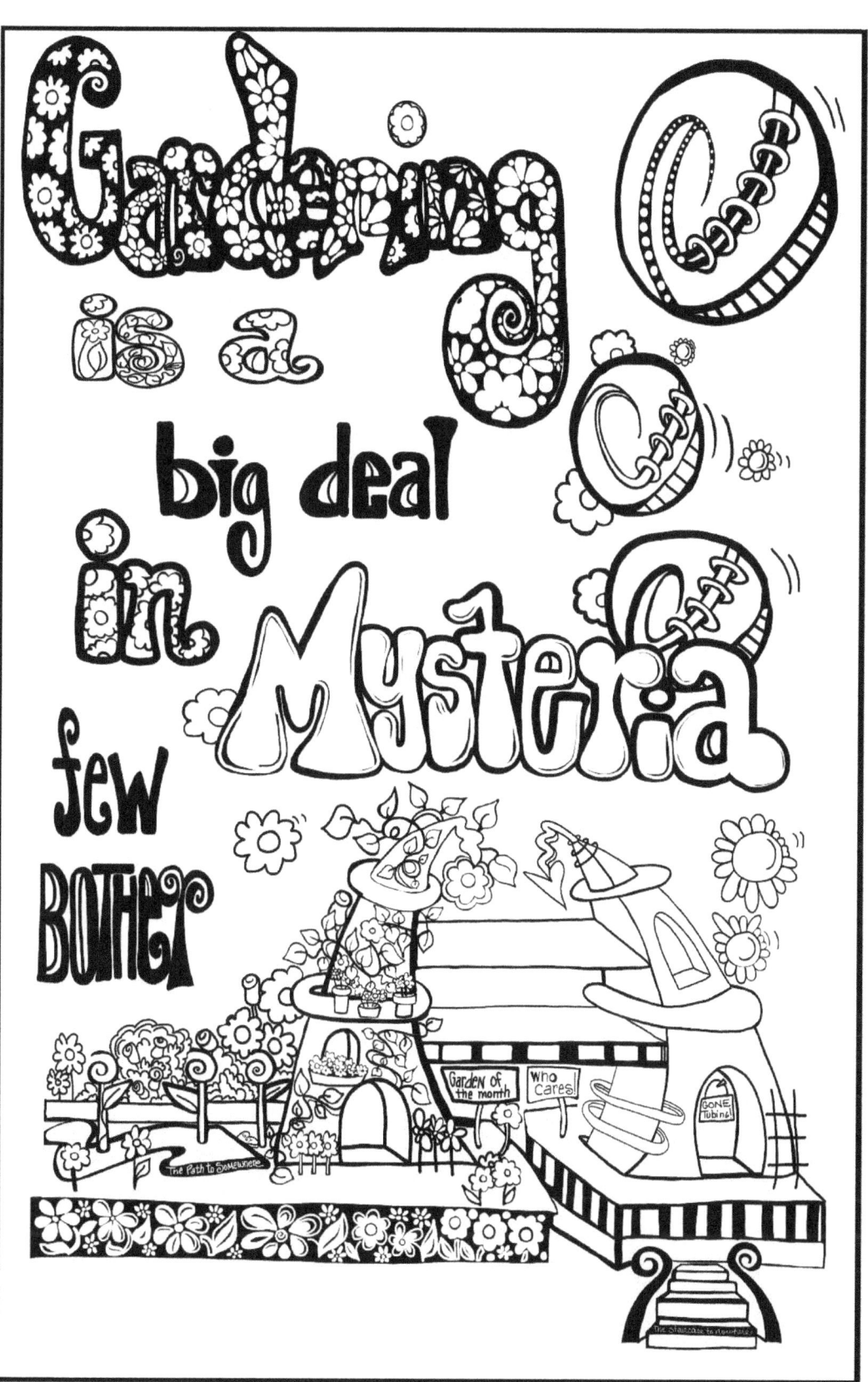

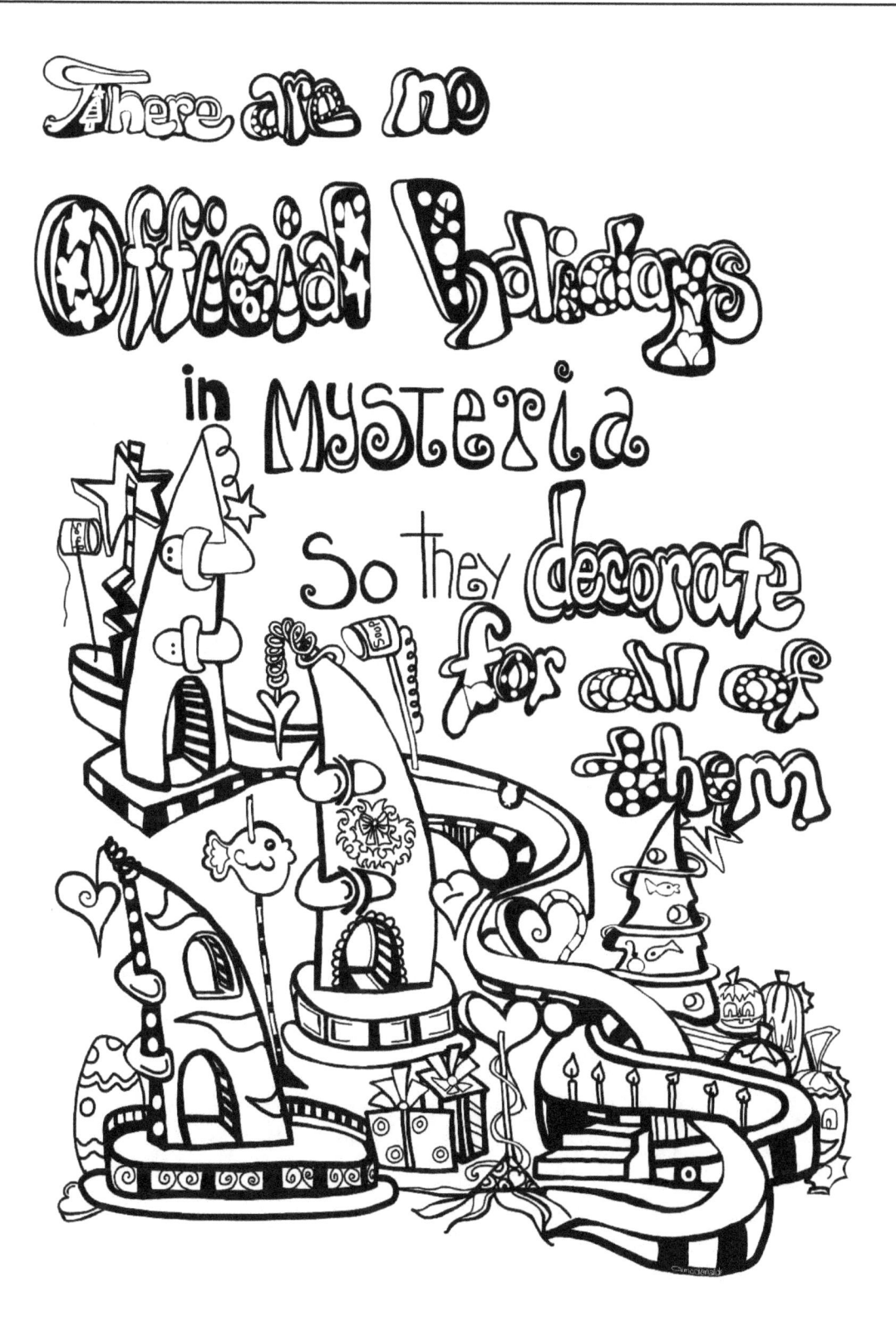

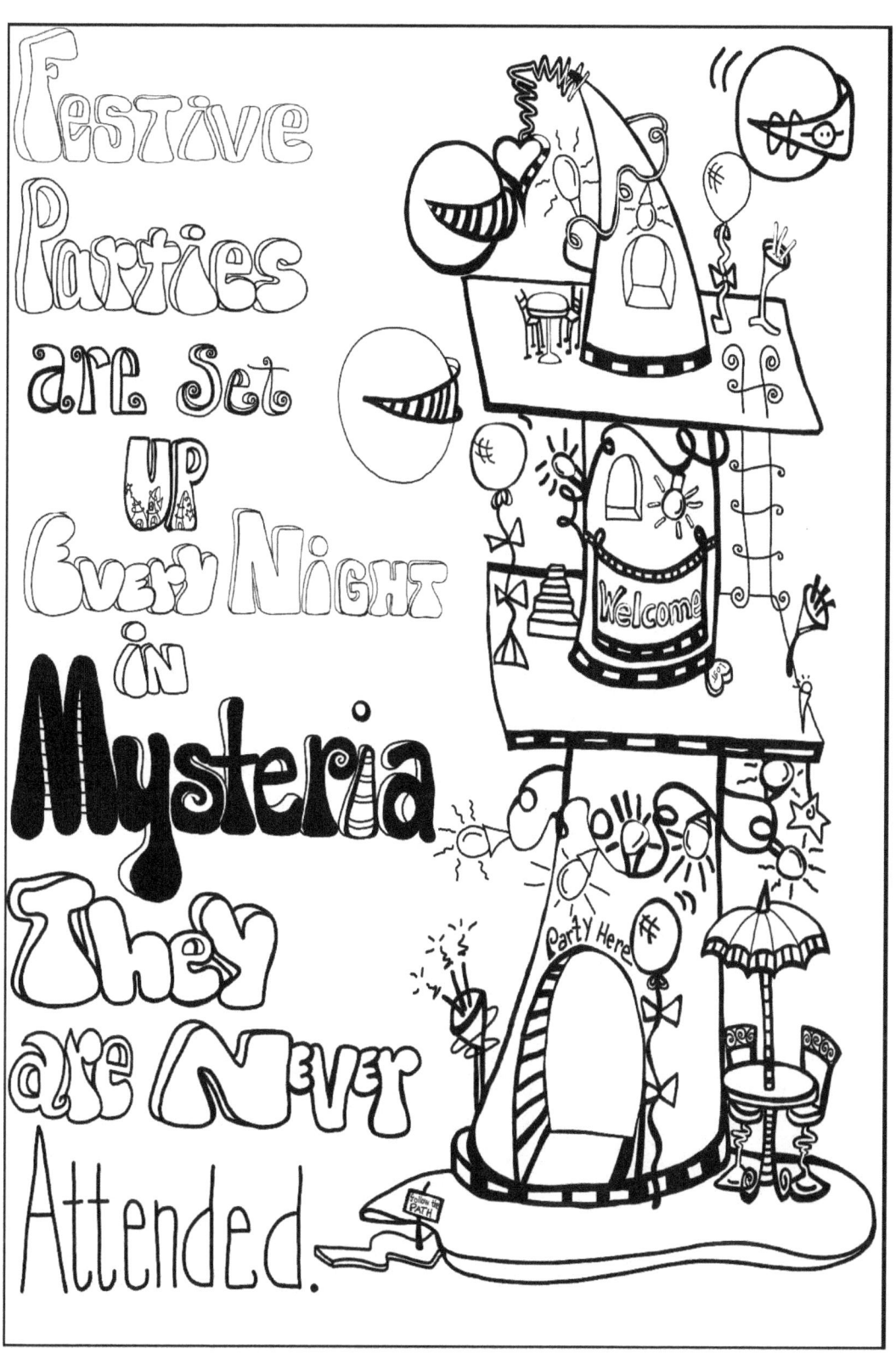

Festive Parties are Set Up Every Night in Mysteria They are Never Attended.

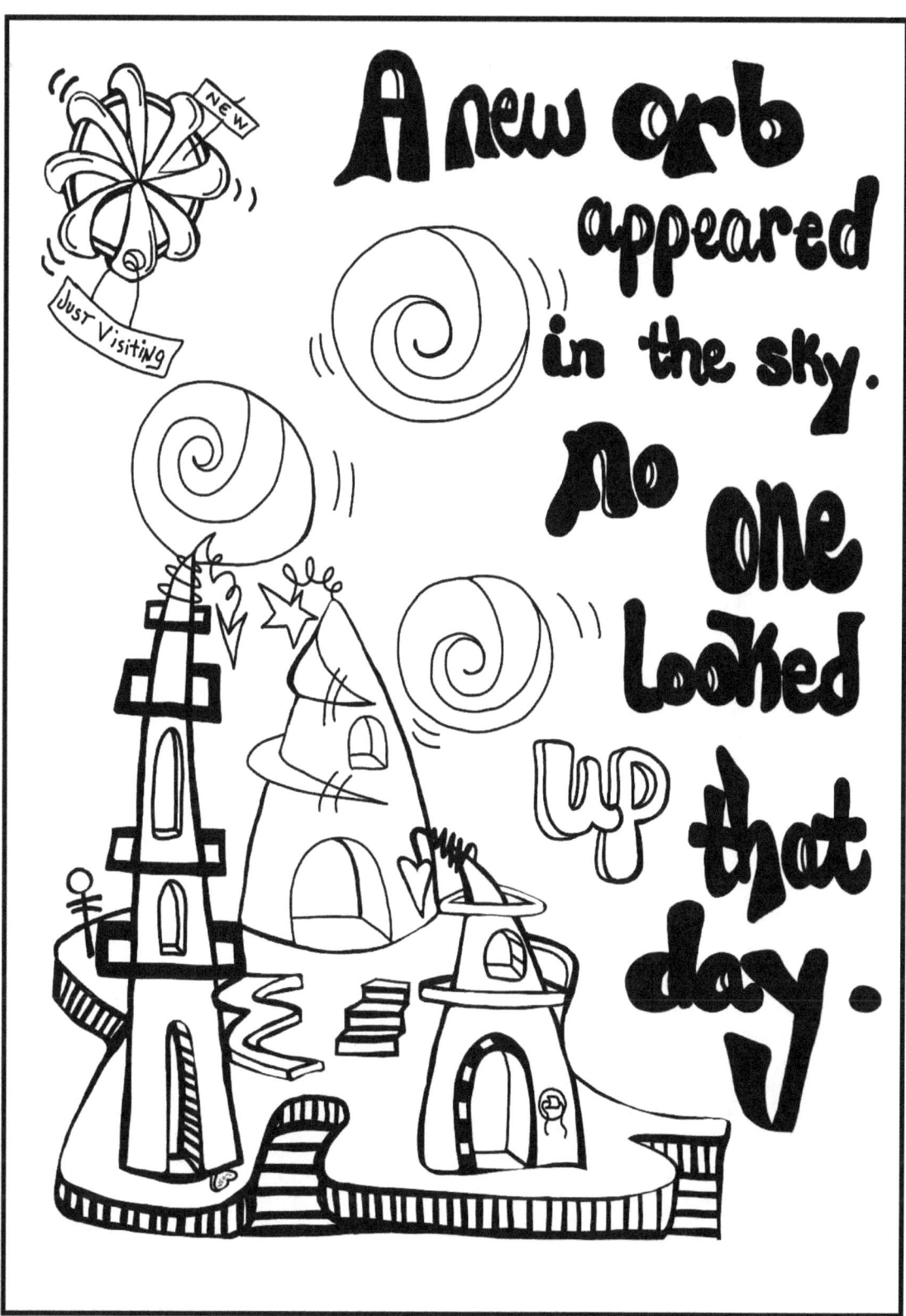

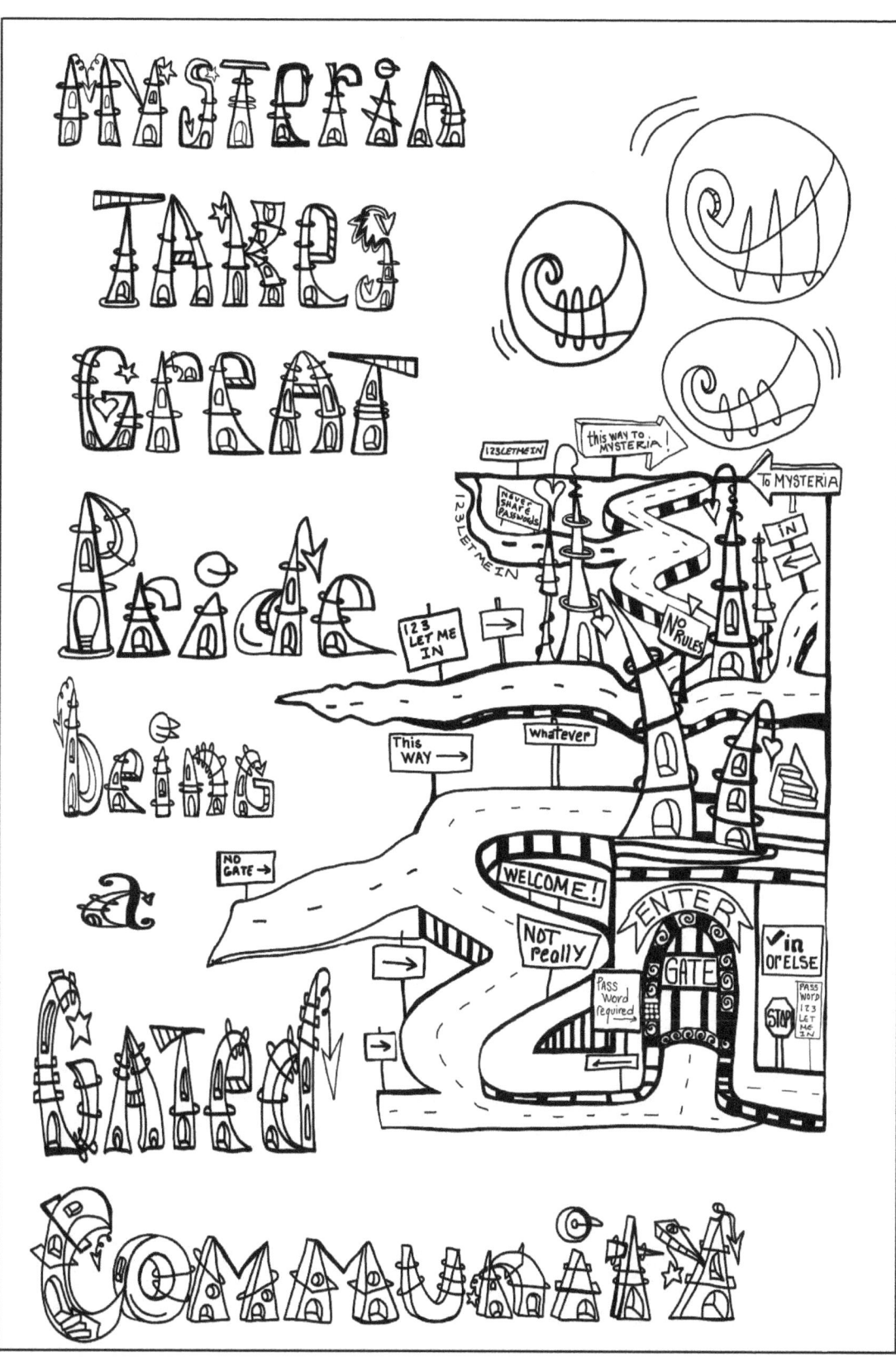

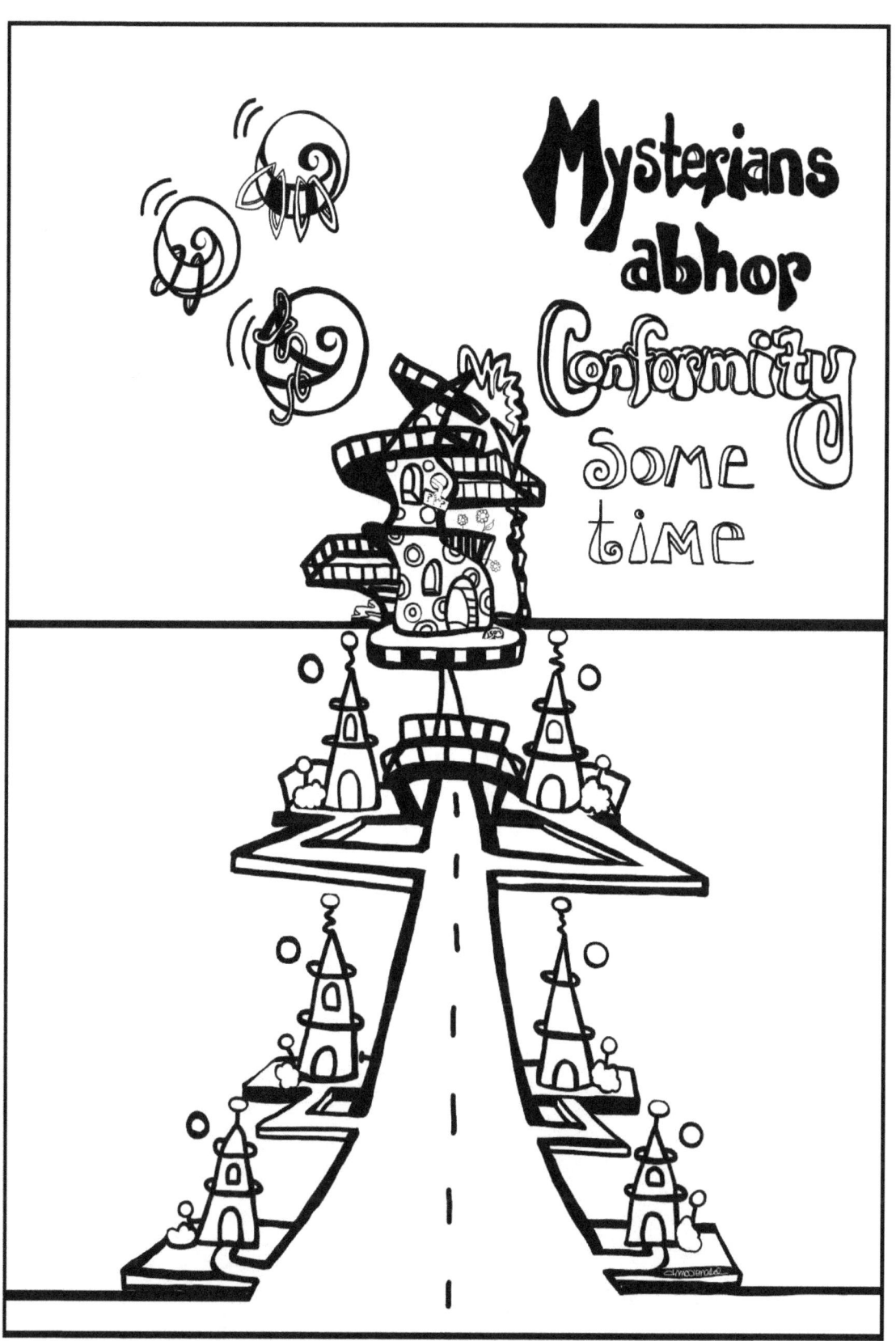

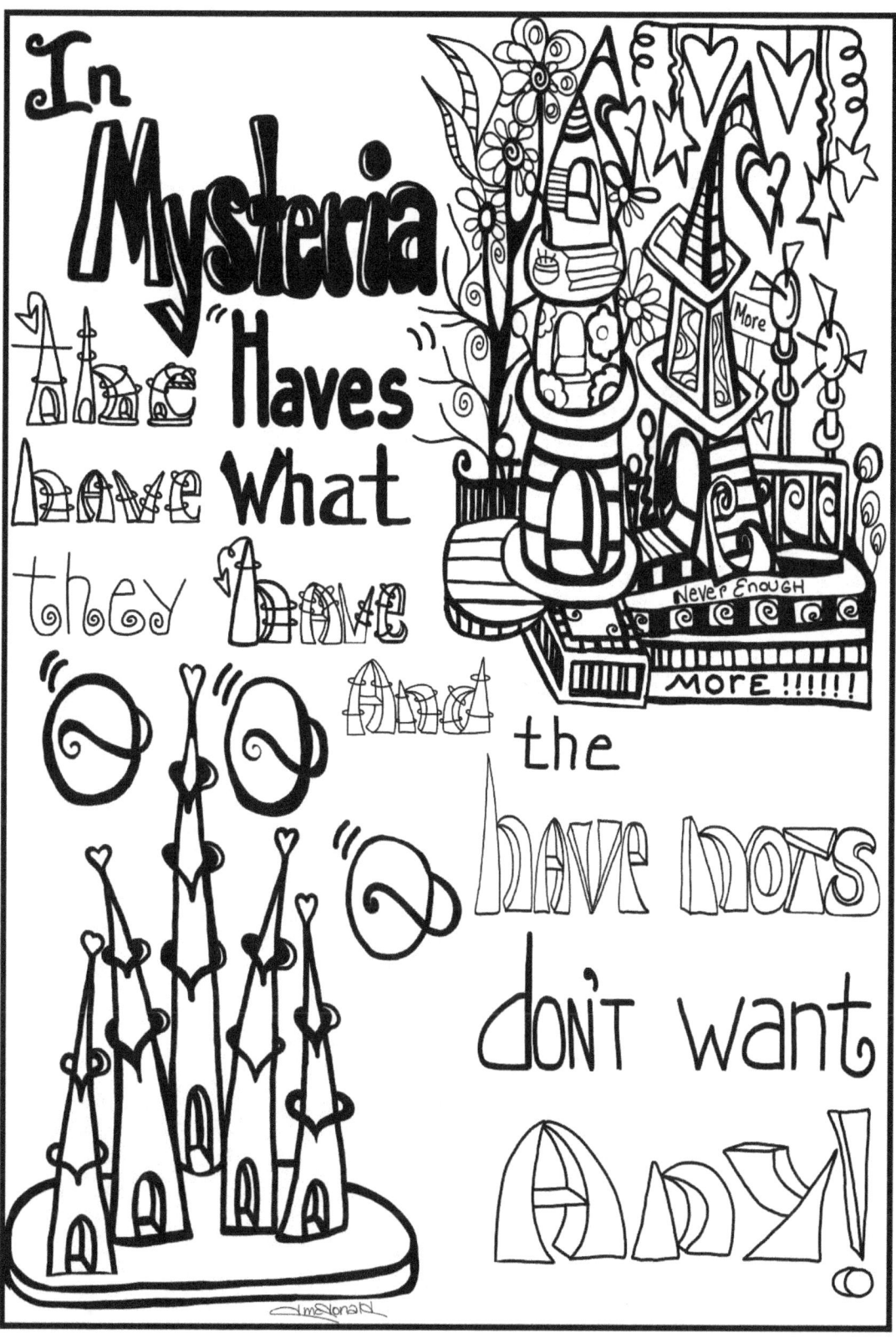

One day Vote for "me" SIGNS SPRUNG UP in MYSTERIA. There has Never been an ELECTION in Mysteria and no One recalled ever meeting "ME"

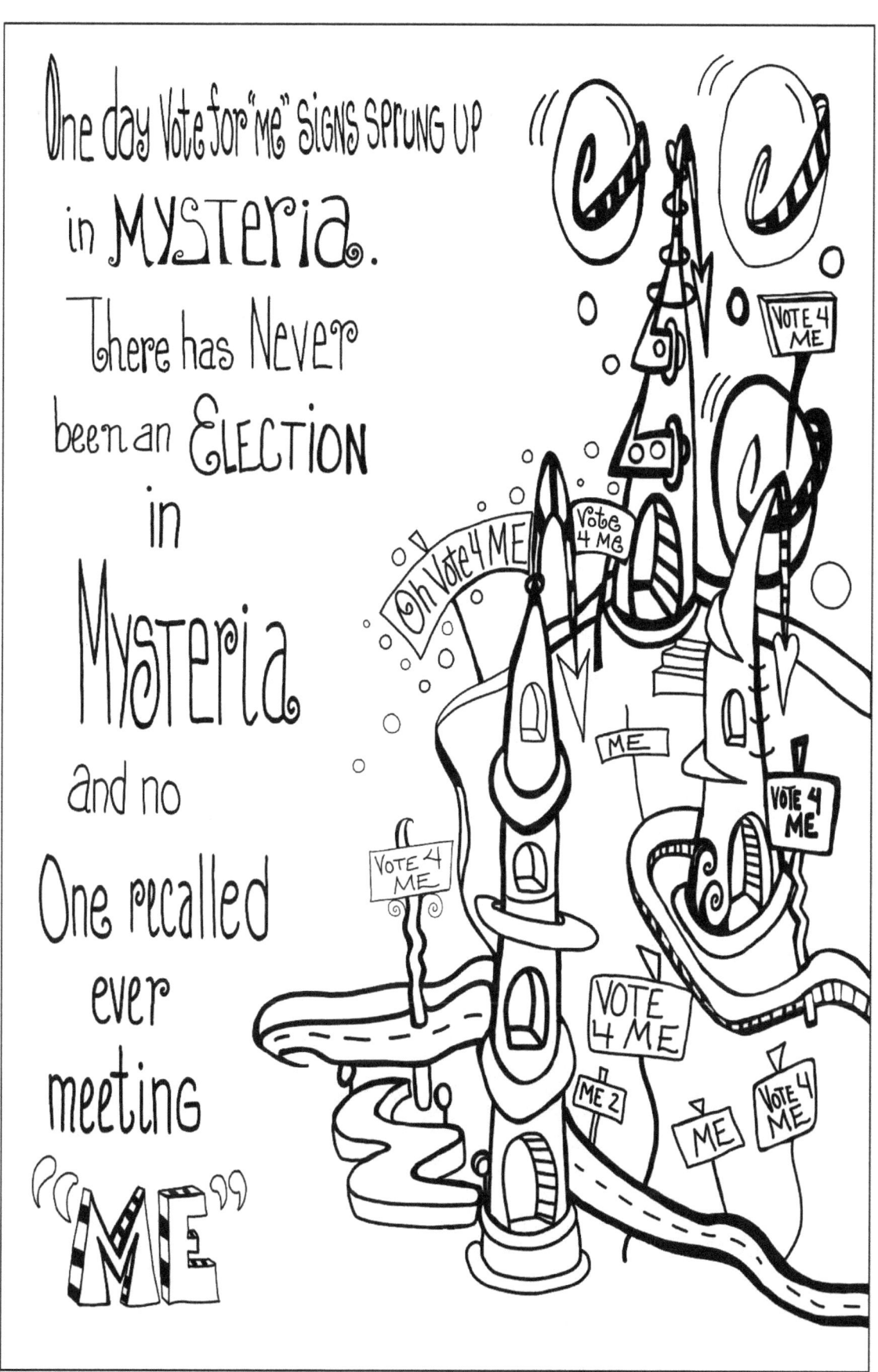

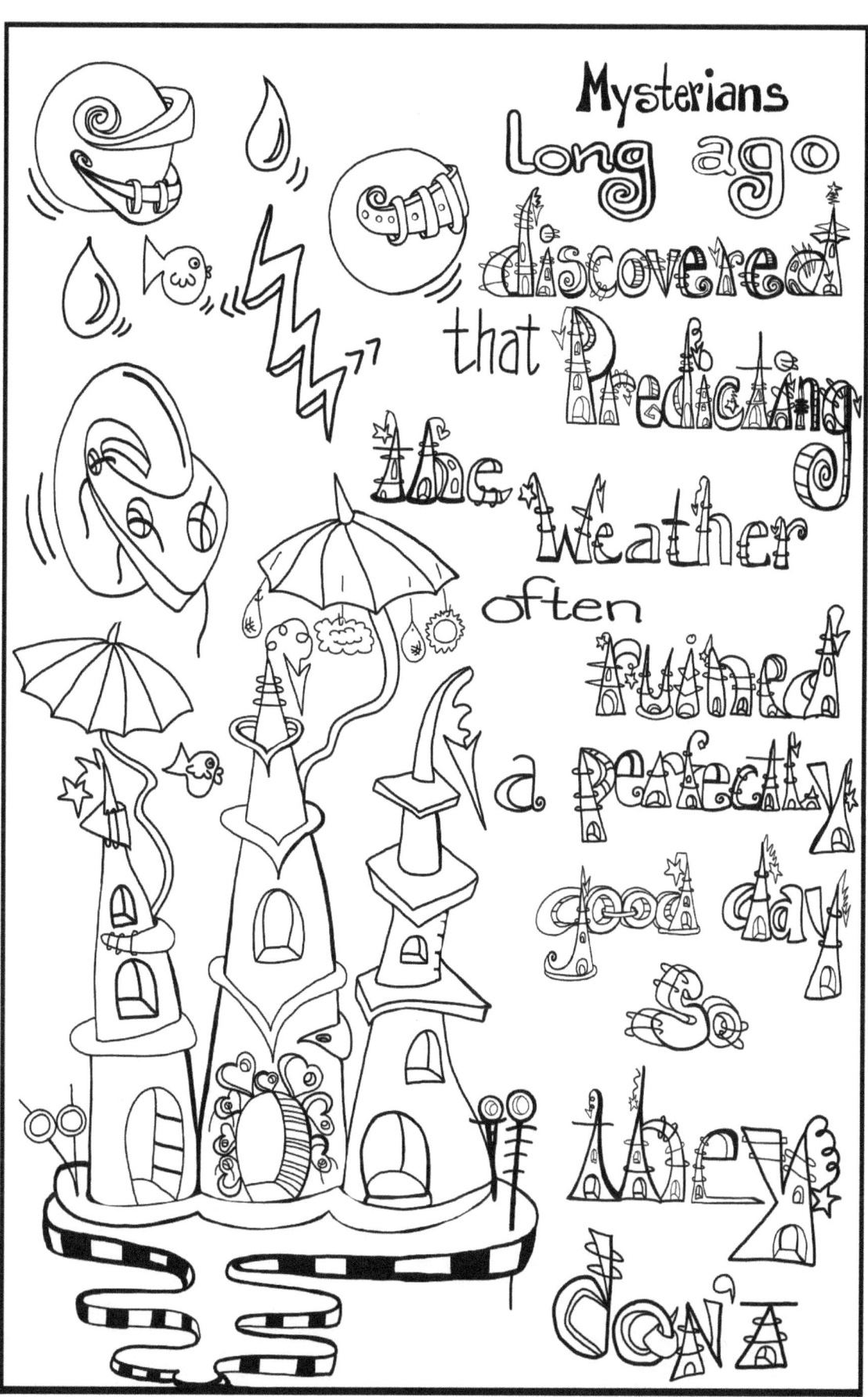

Mysterians

Long ago discovered that Predicting the weather often ruined a perfectly good day so they don't

Some one mentioned the idea of a city-wide garage sale MYSTERIANS wanted to know more. It was agreed that they had things because they wanted them and COULD NOT IMAGINE not wanting them, because if that were true they would not have these things!

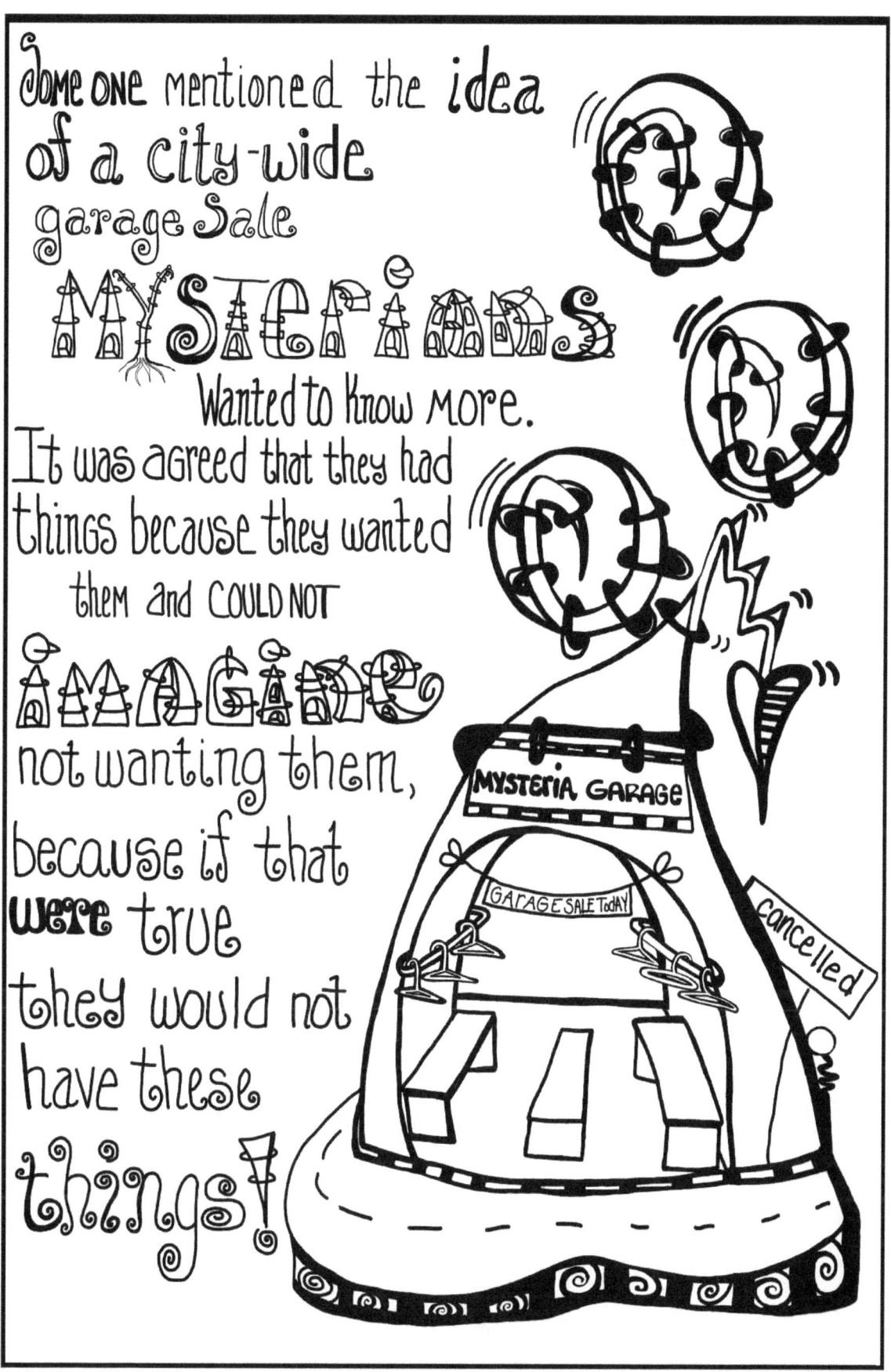

MYSTERIA GARAGE

GARAGE SALE TODAY

cancelled

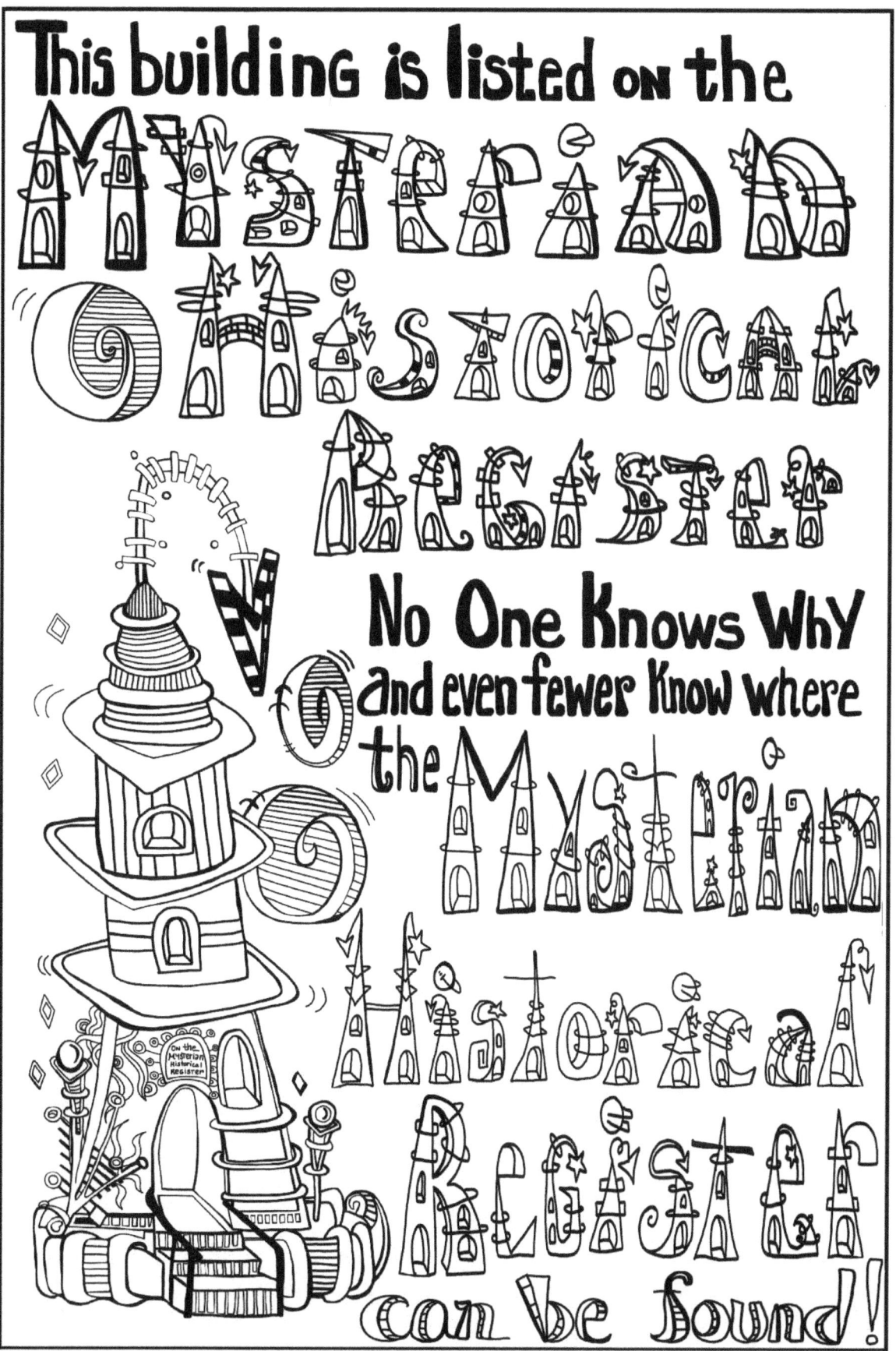

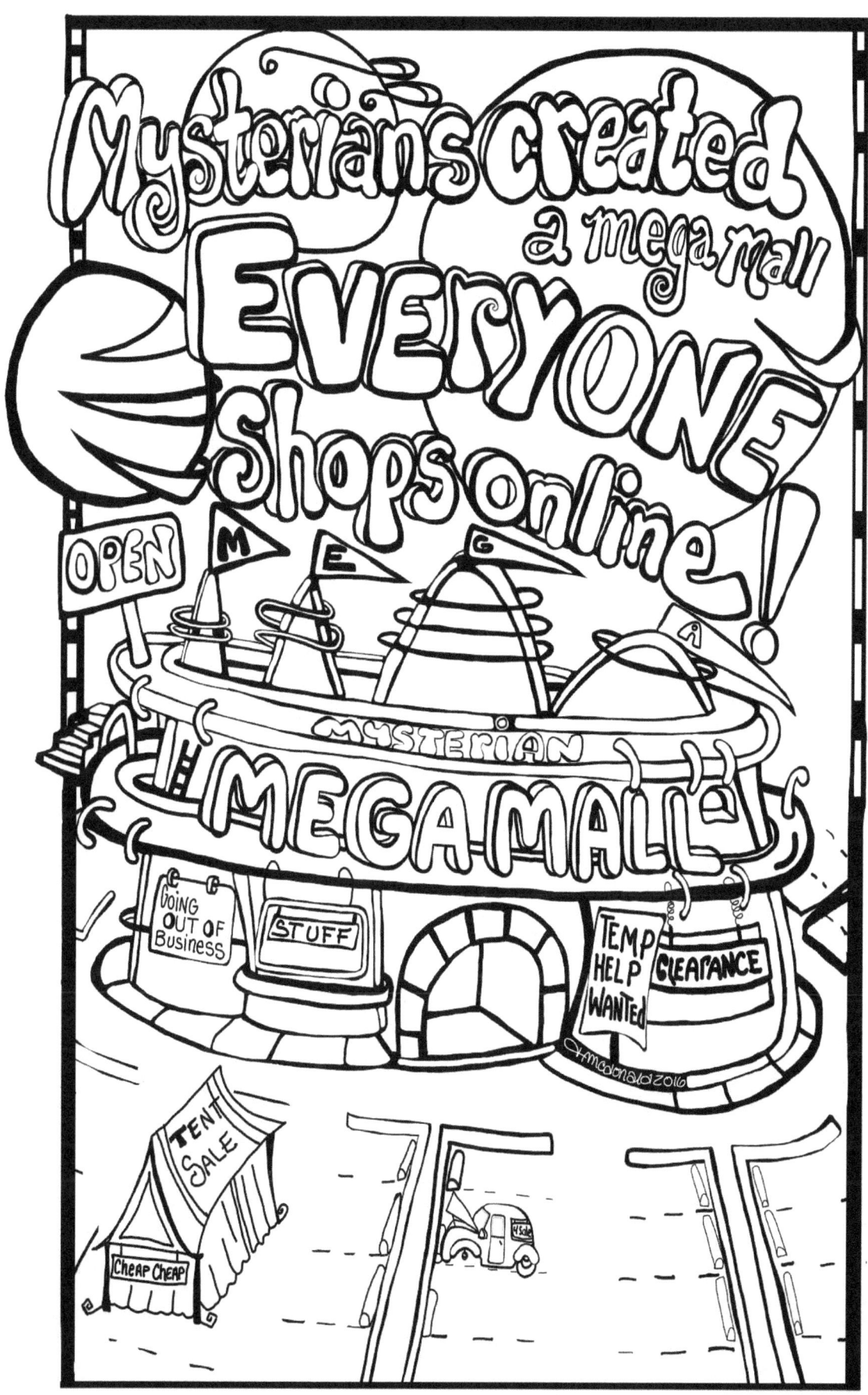

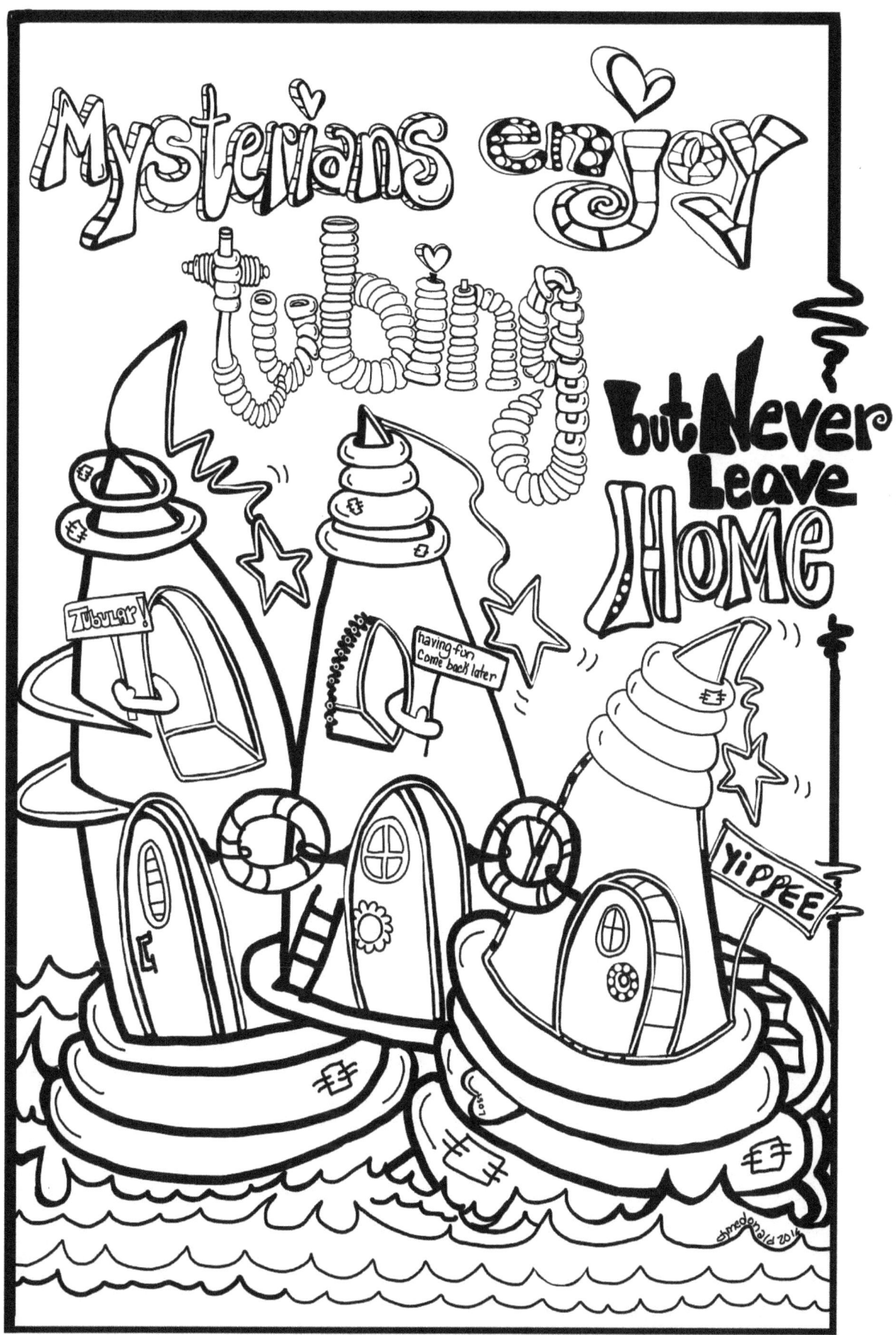

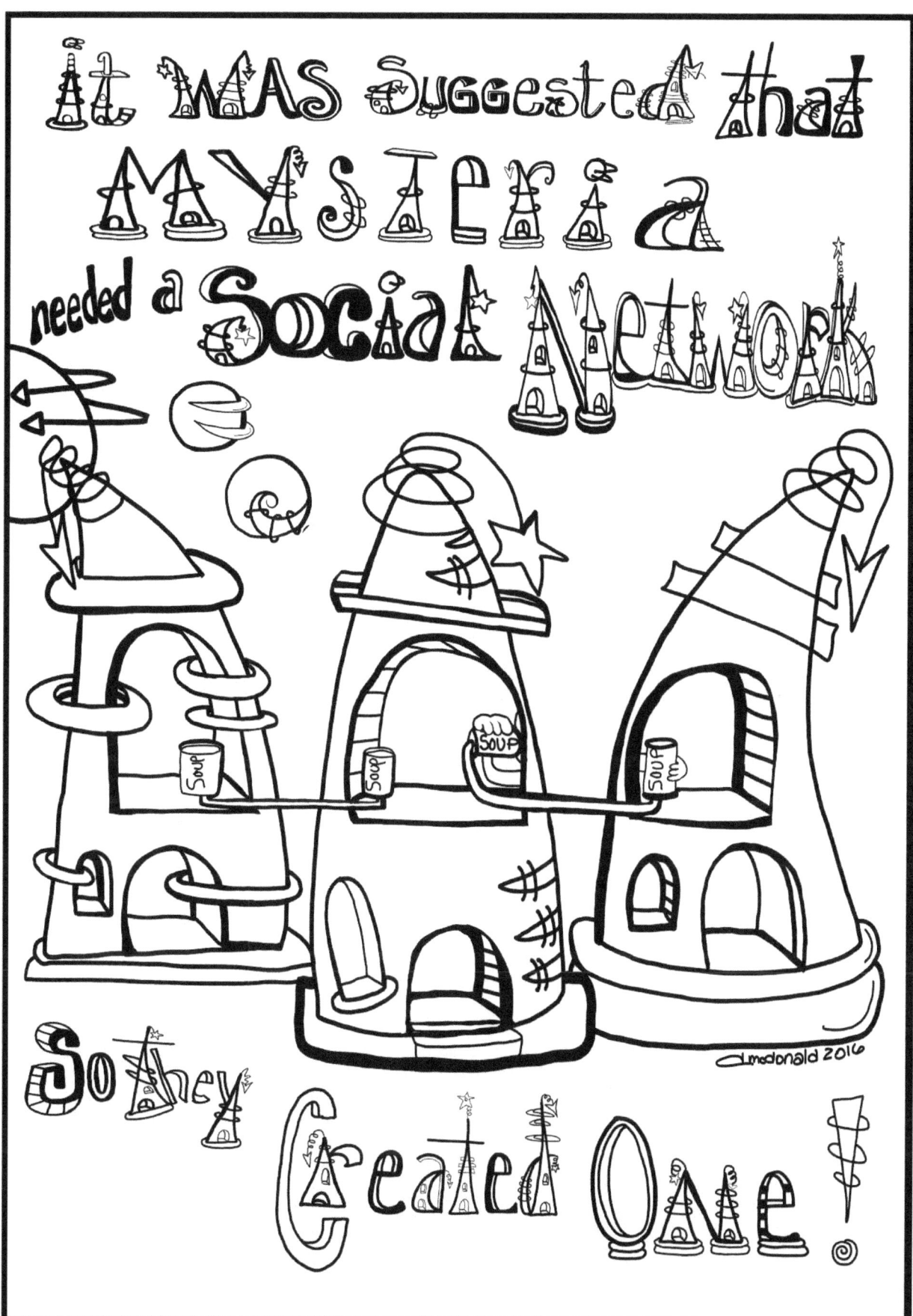

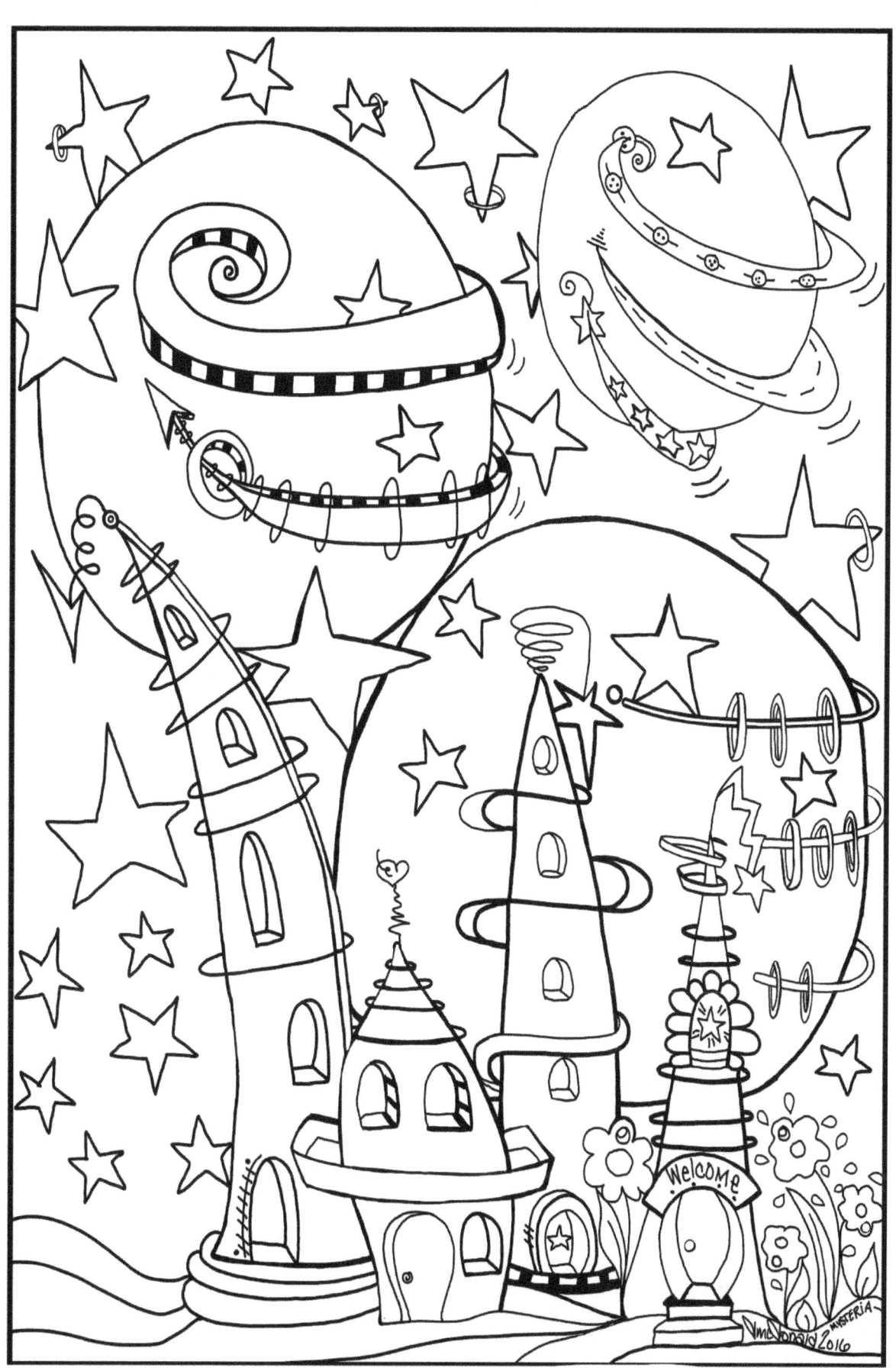

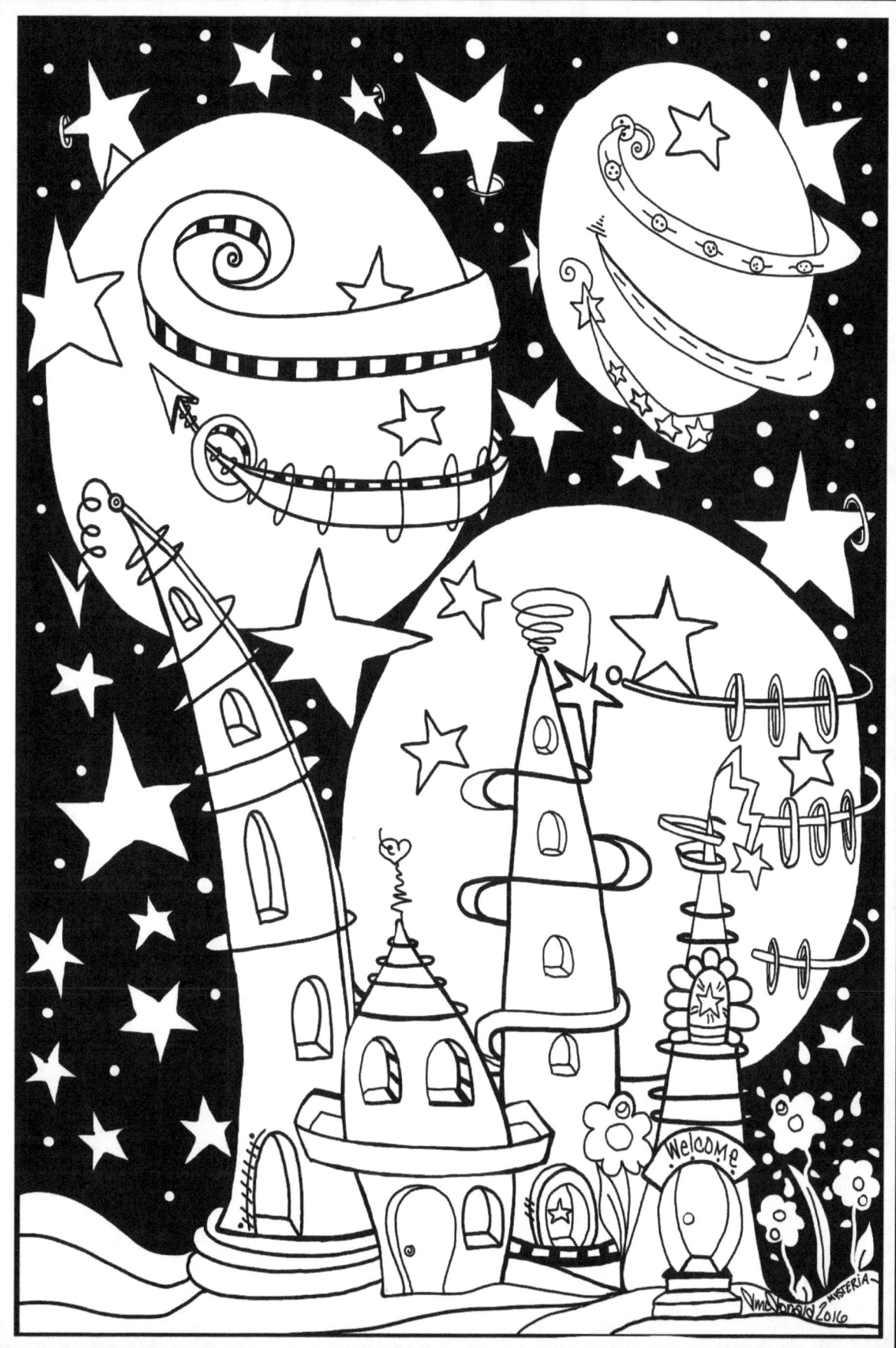

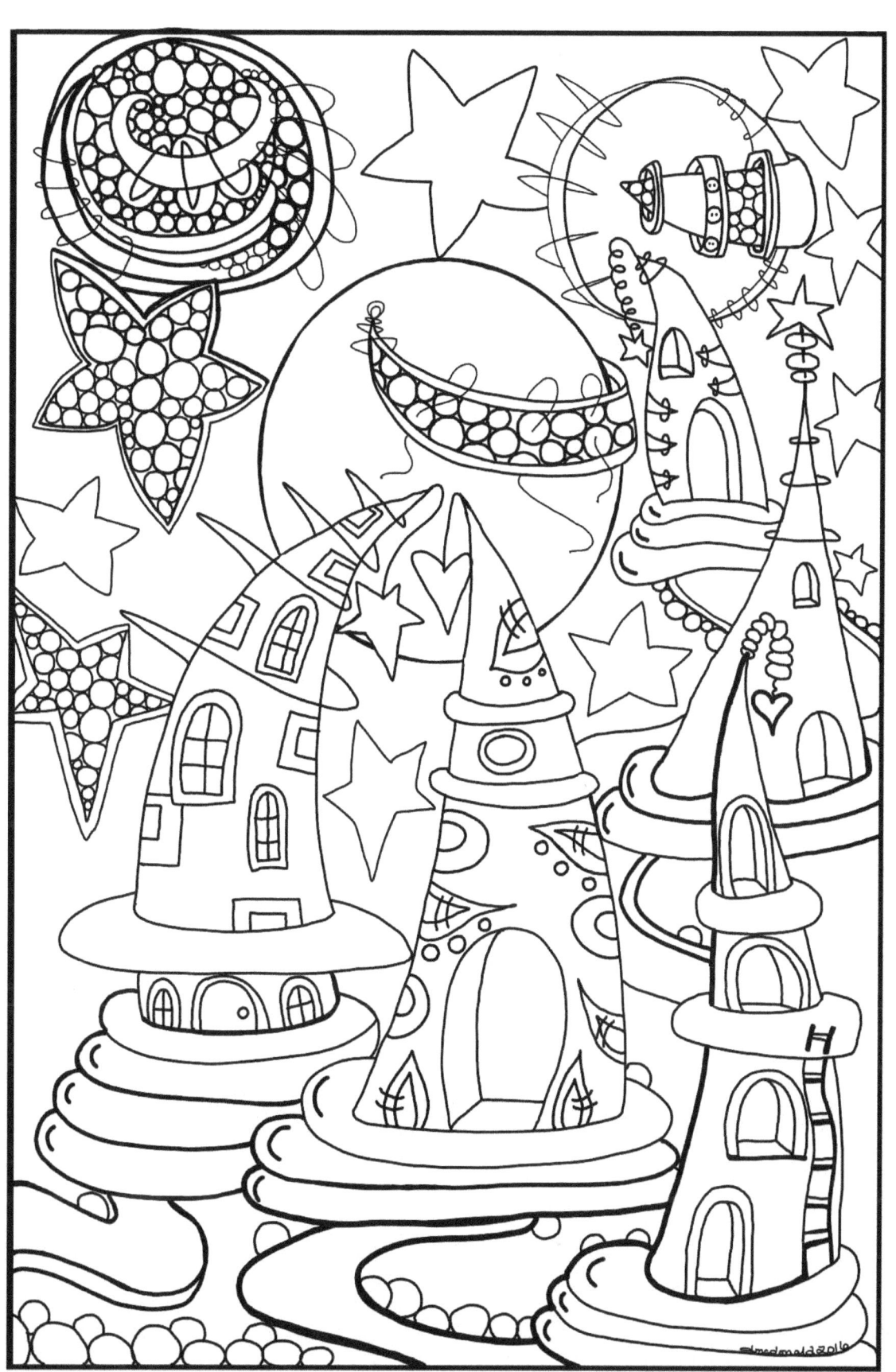

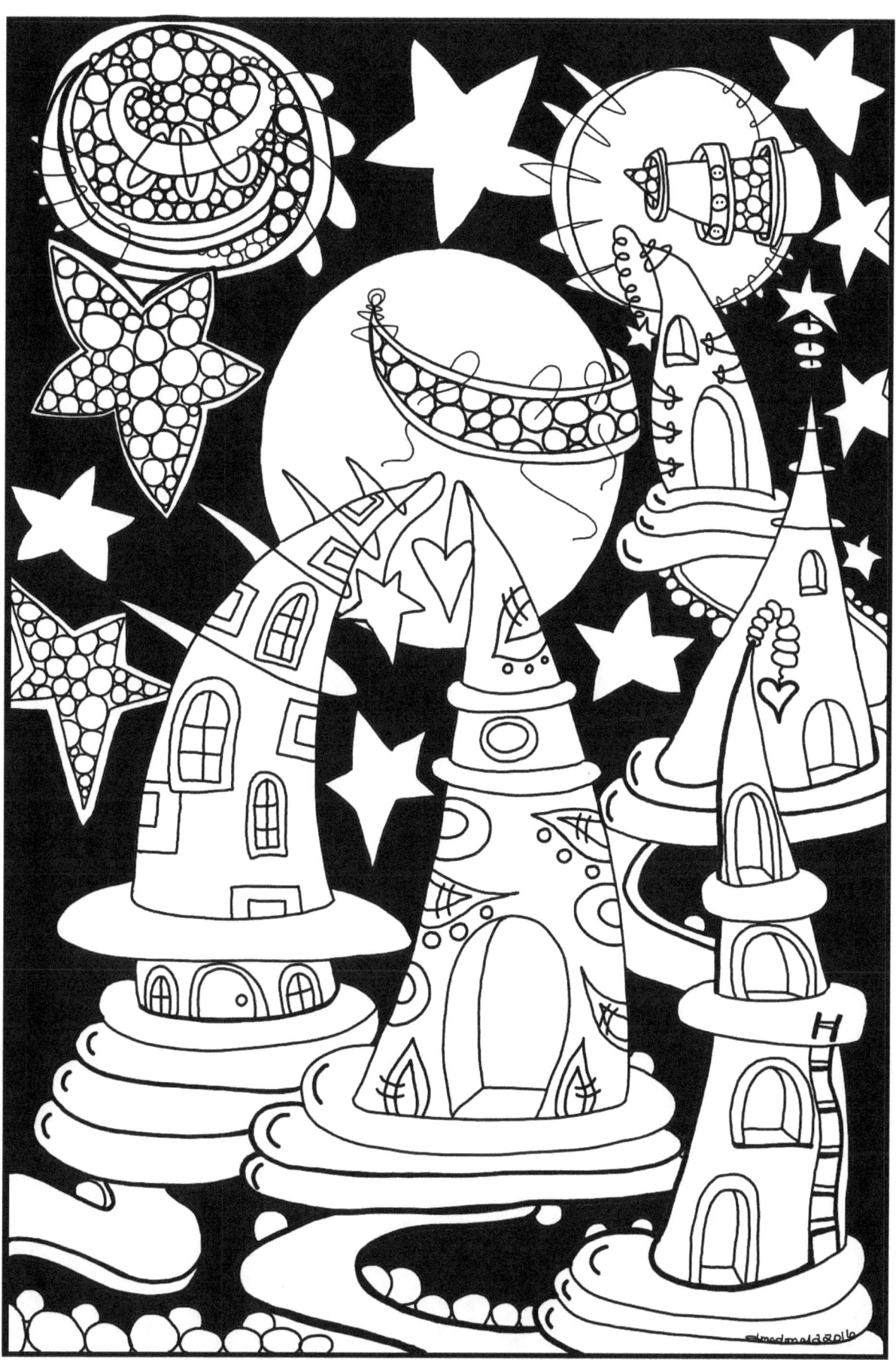

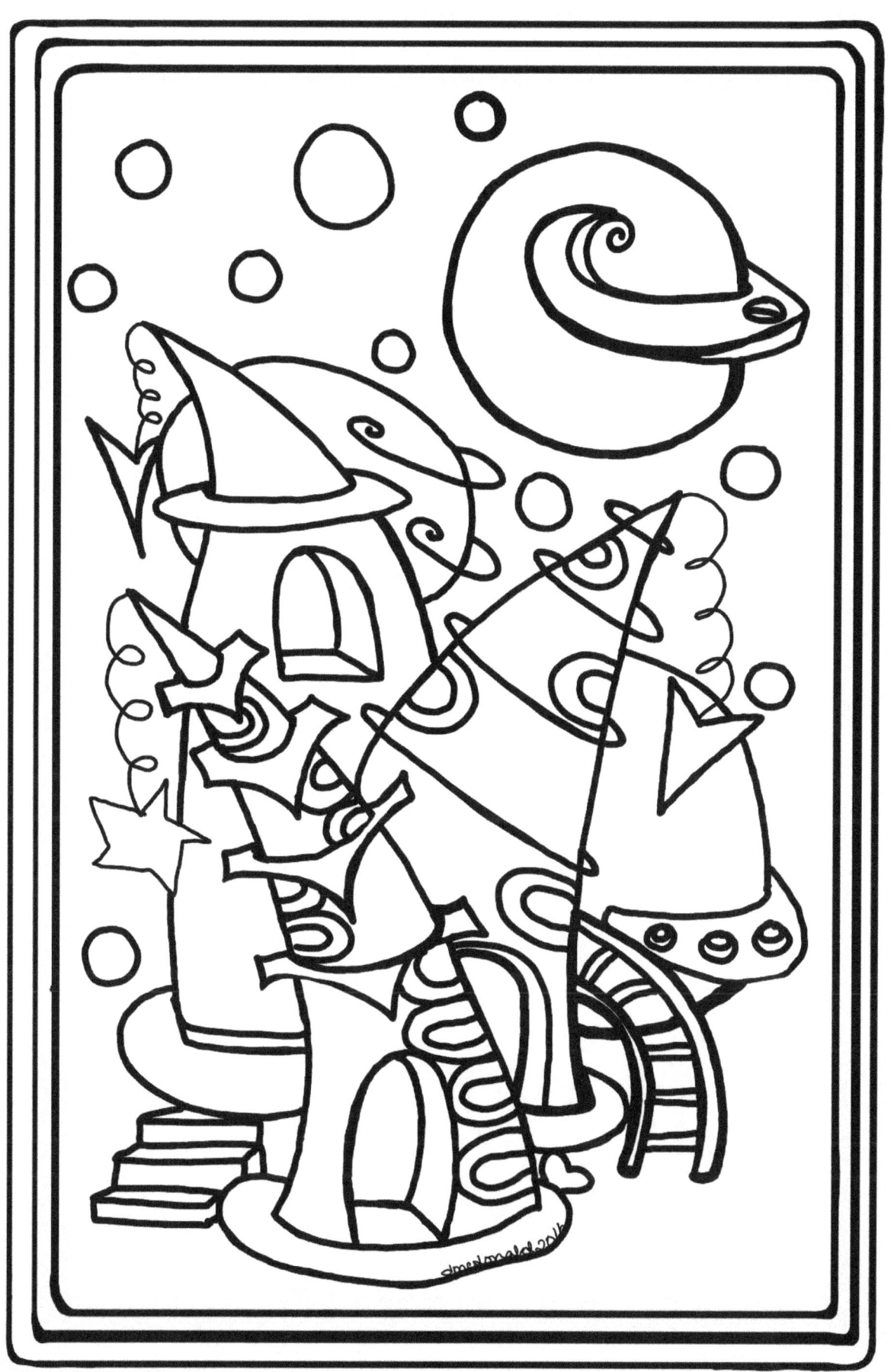

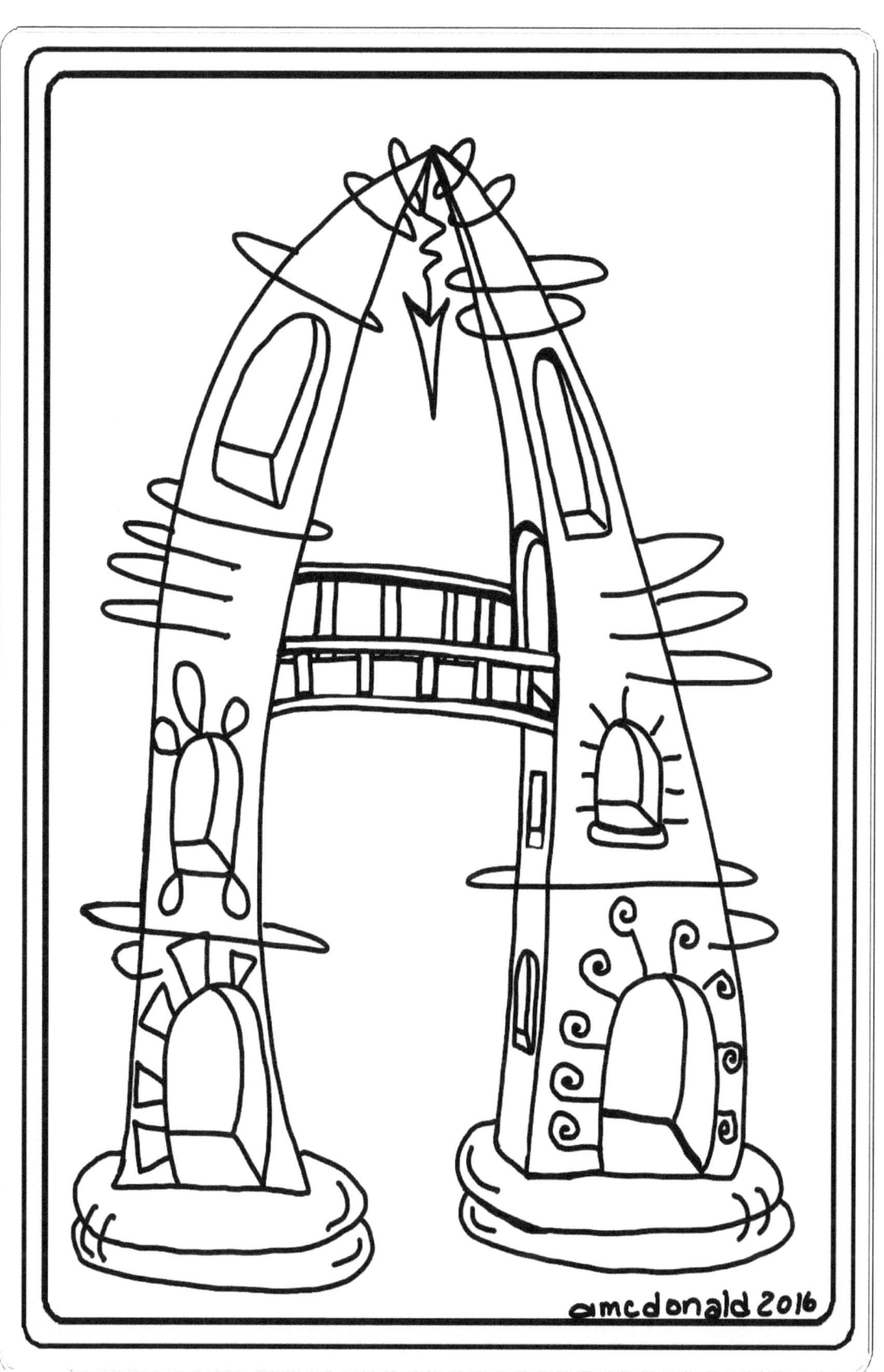

amcdonald 2016

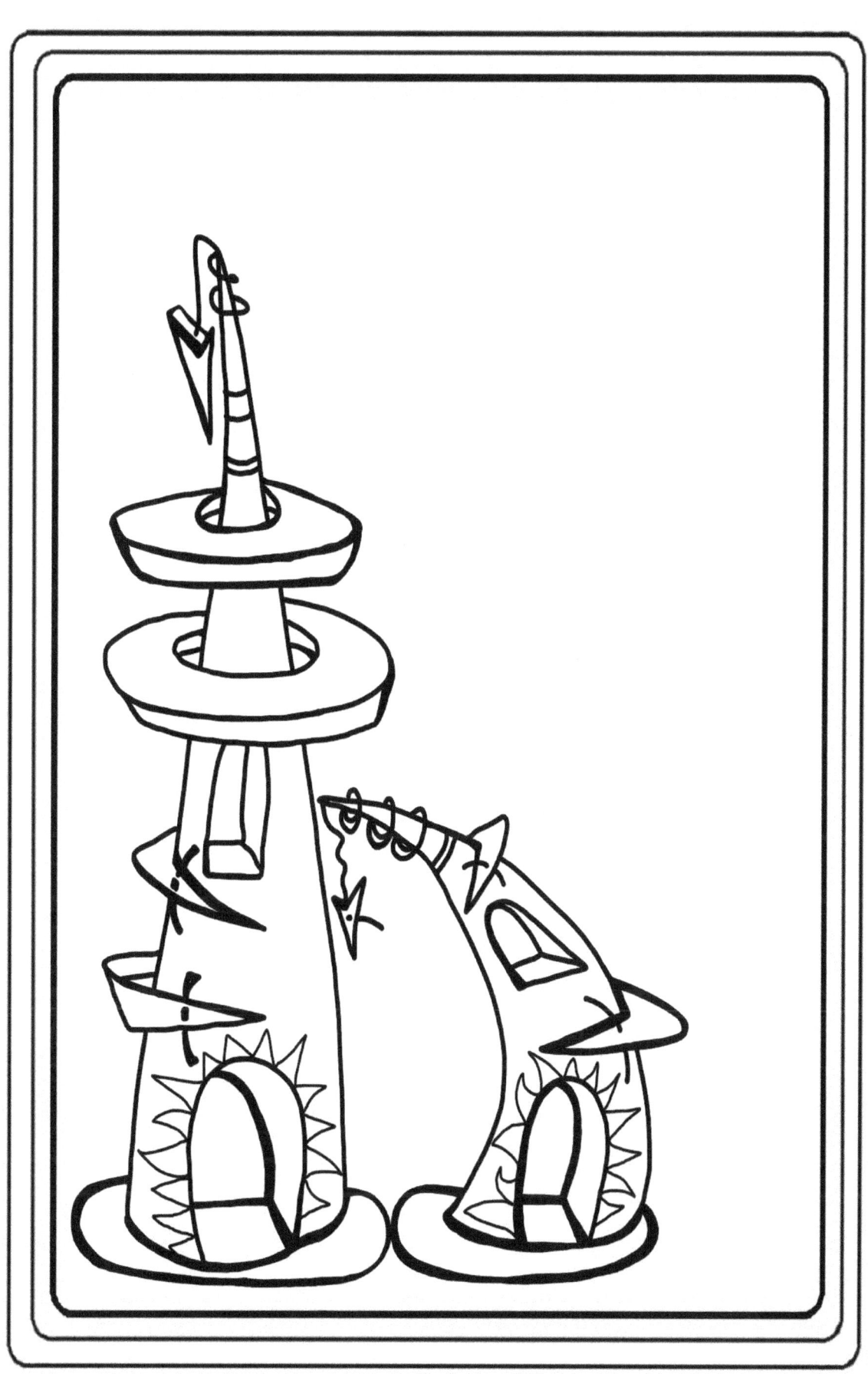

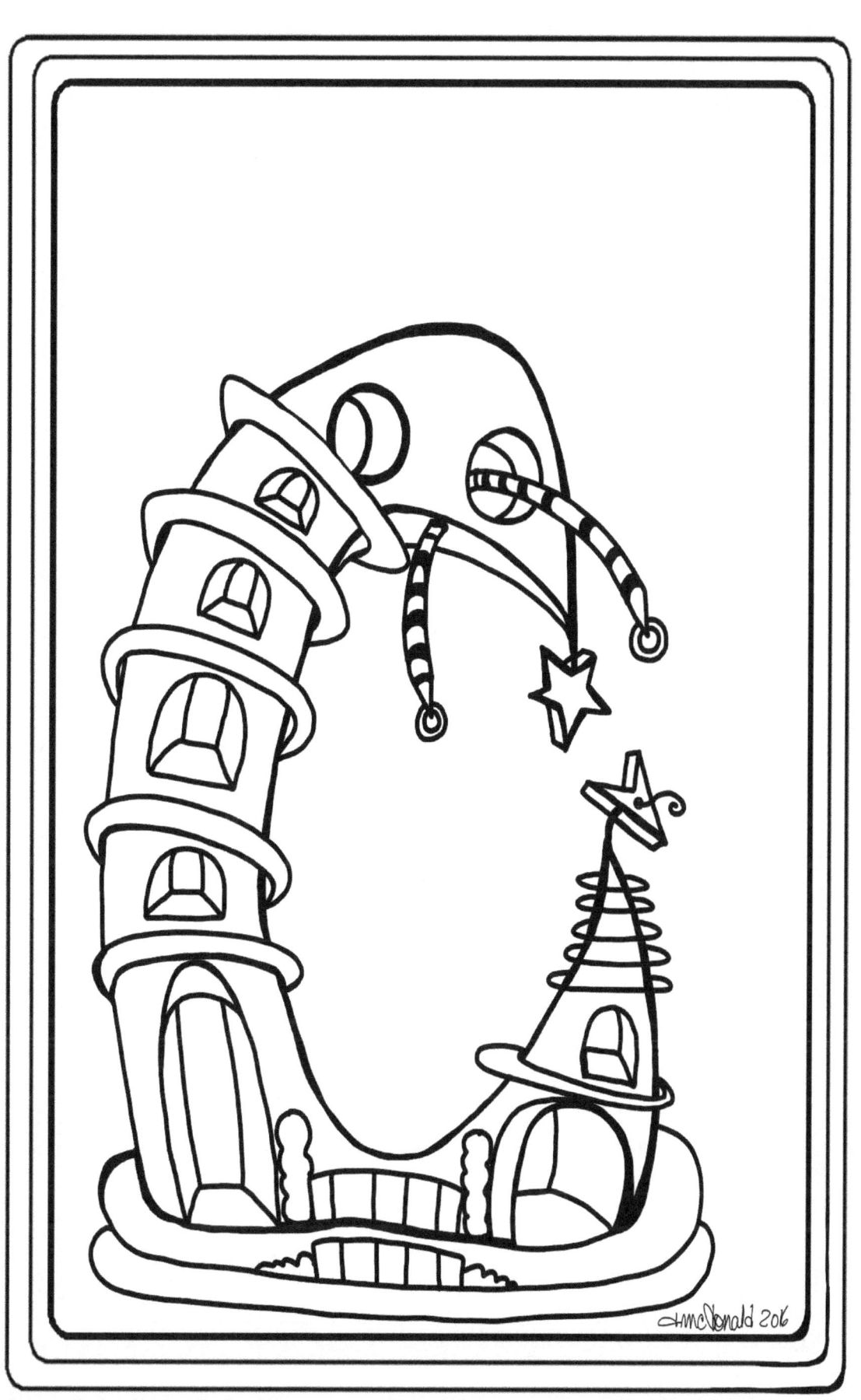

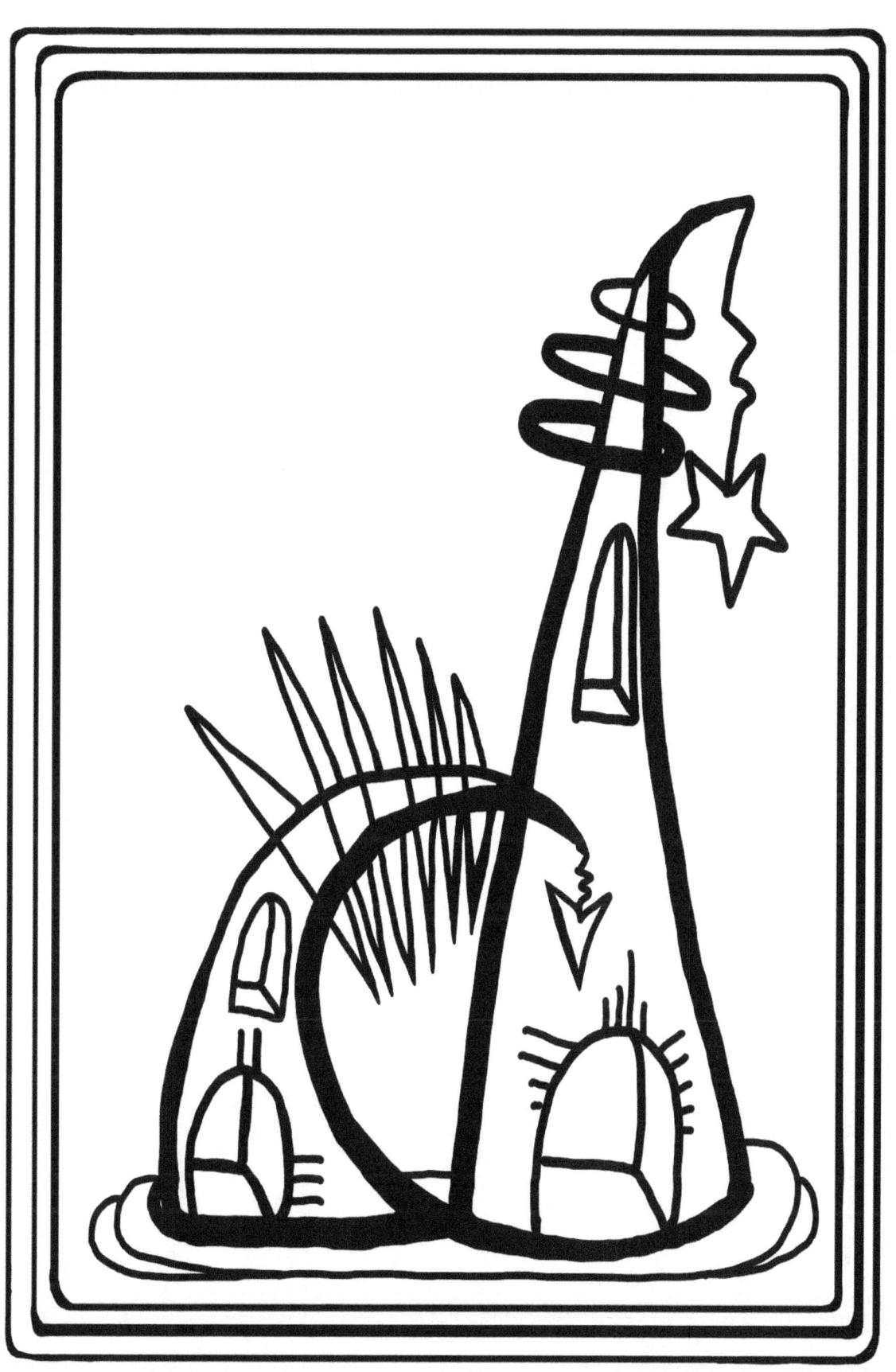

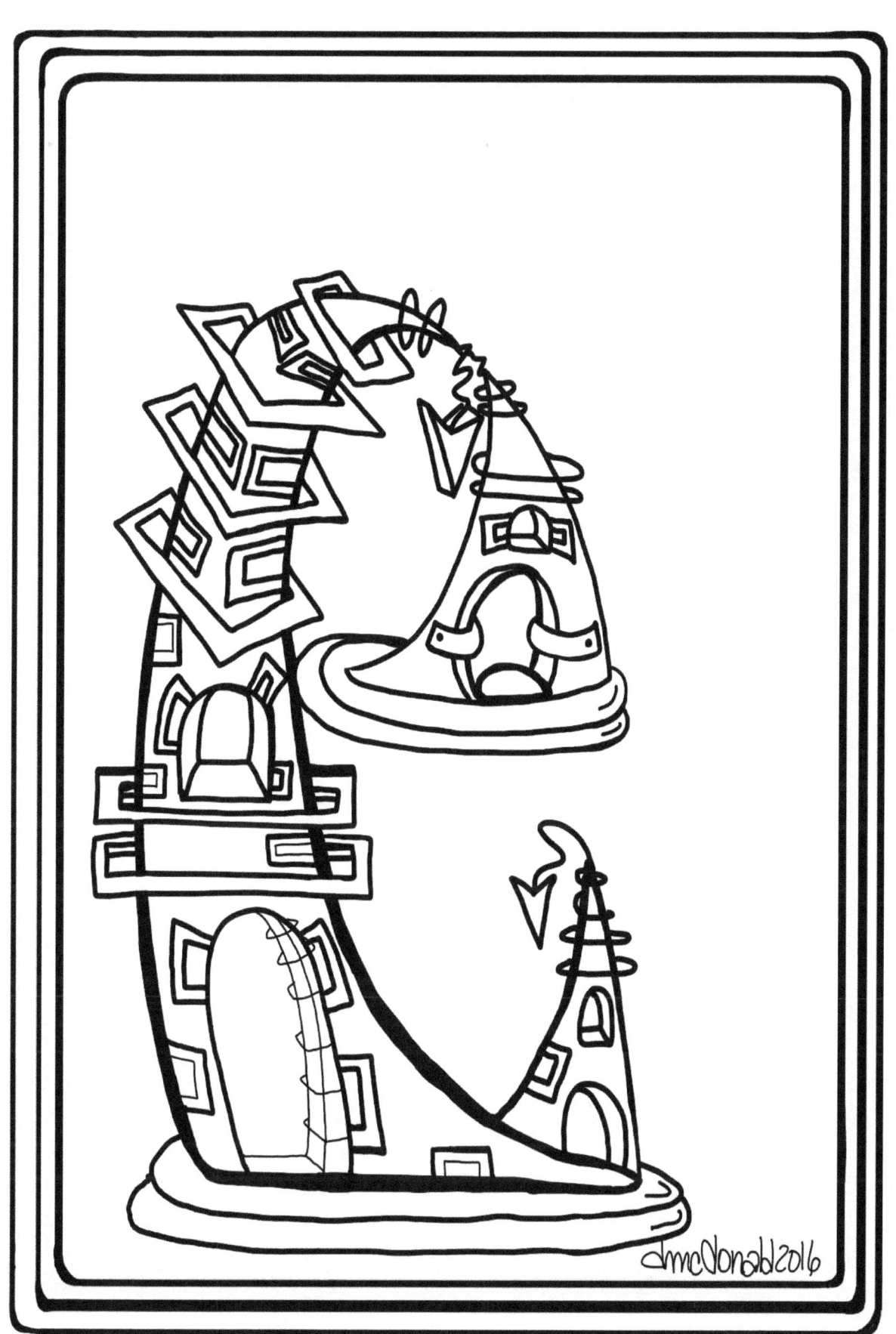

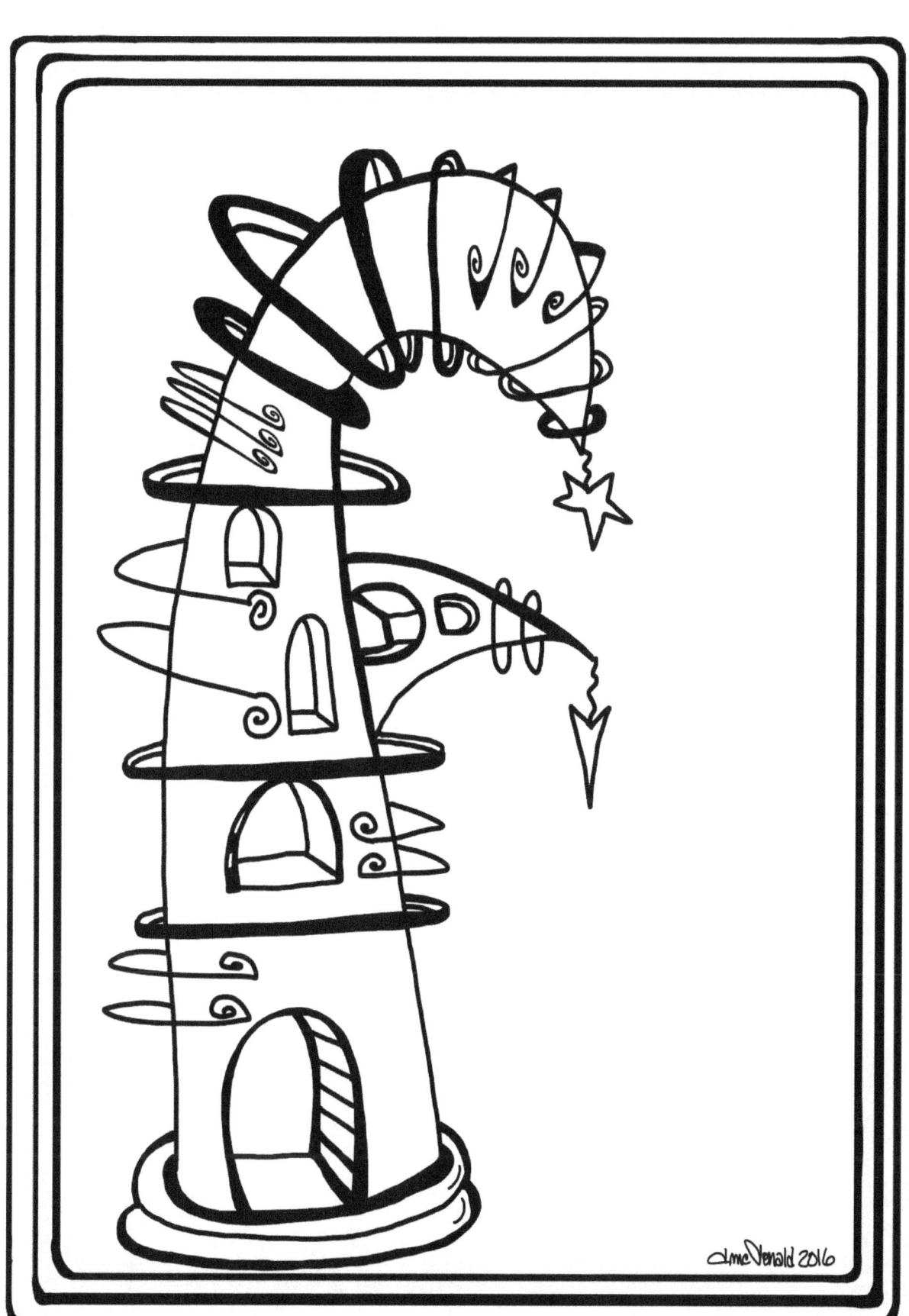

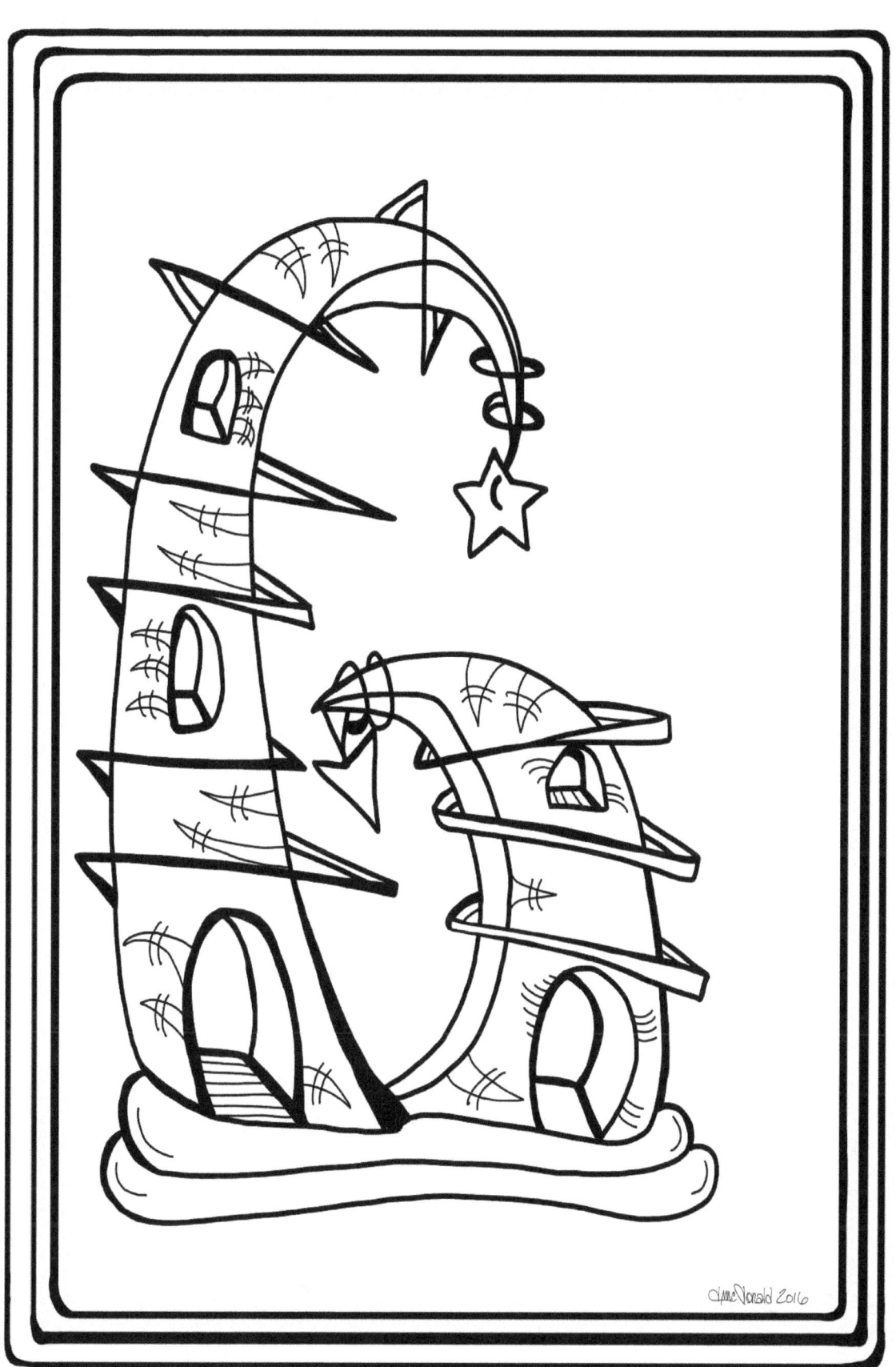

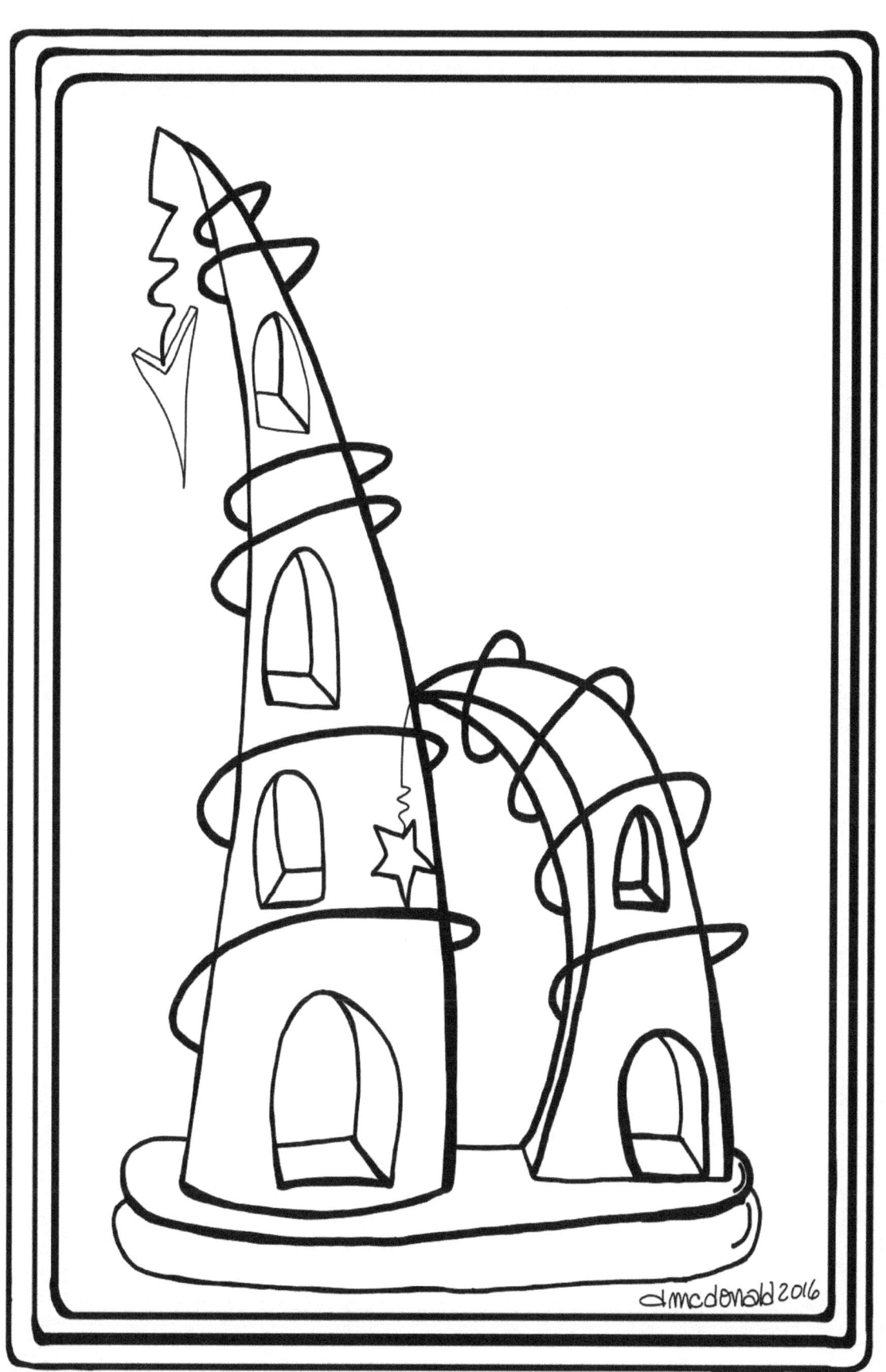

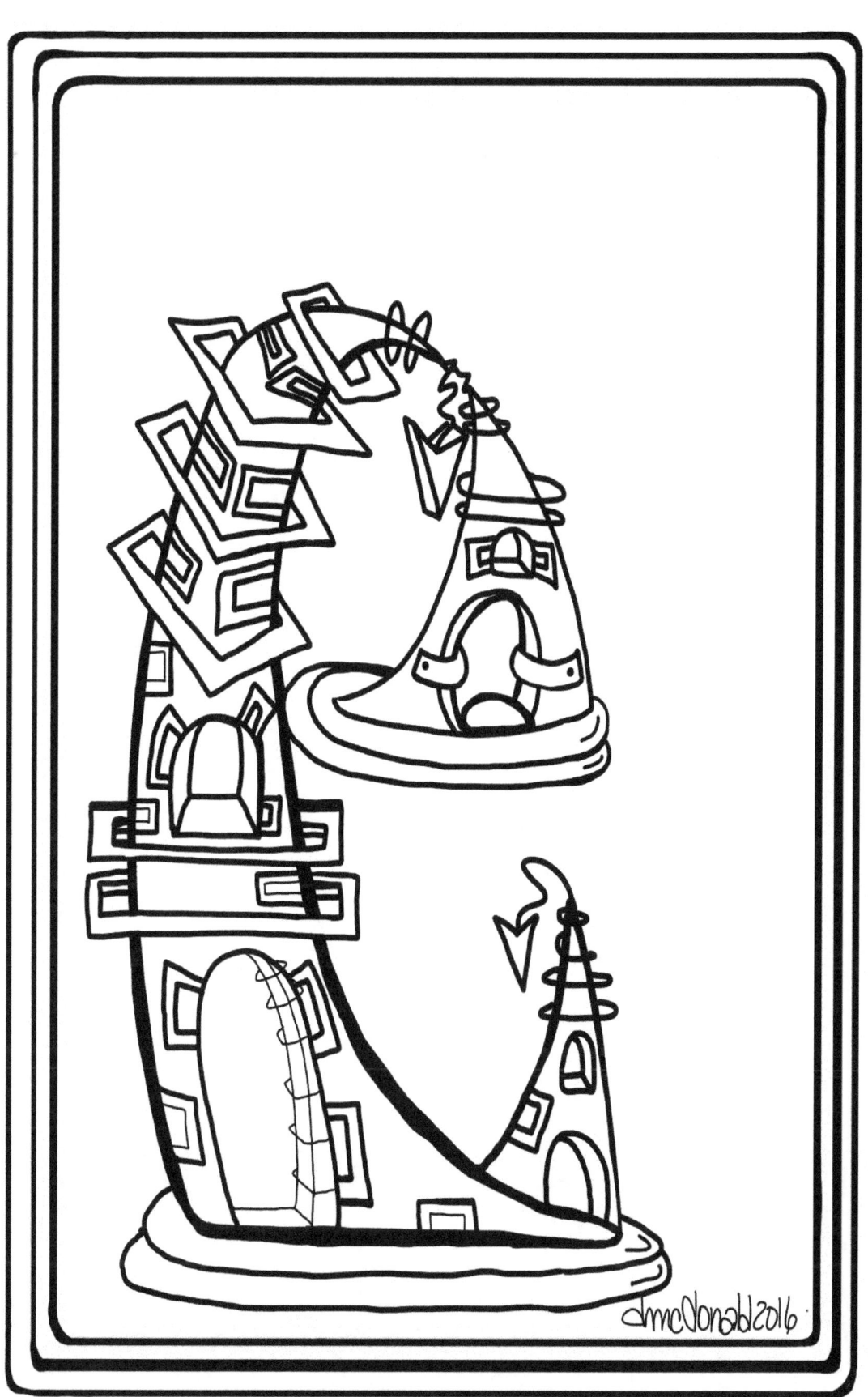

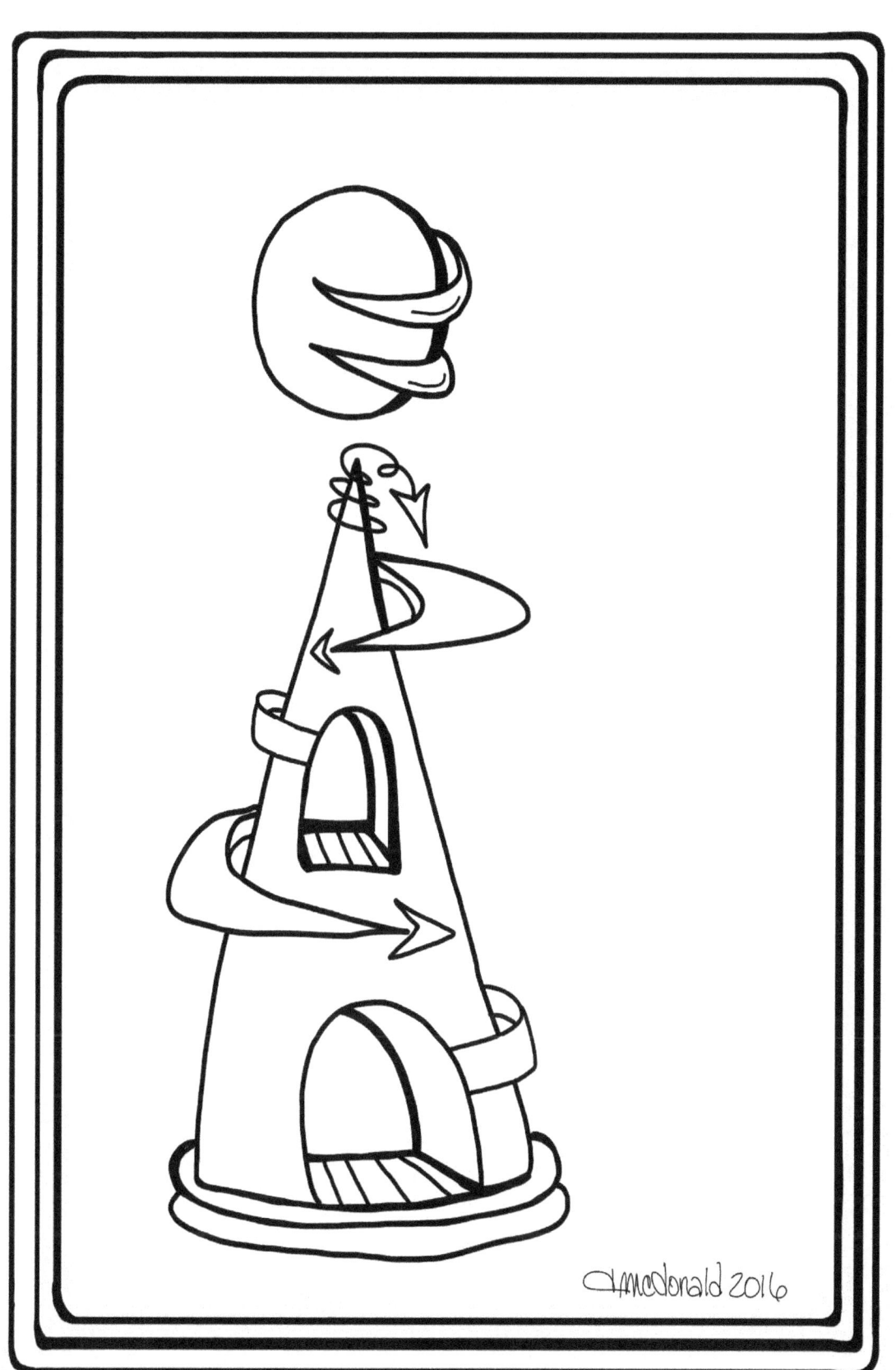

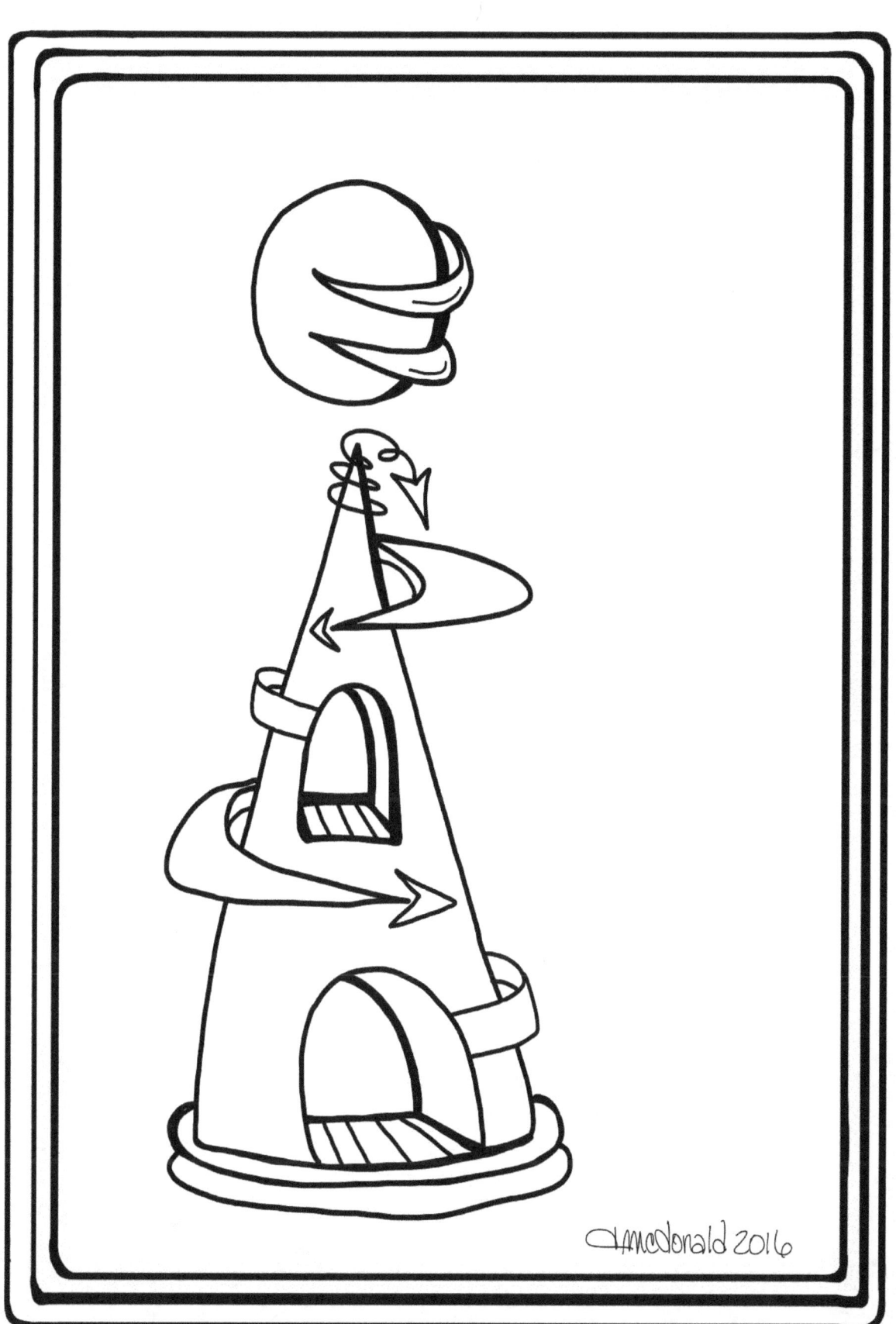

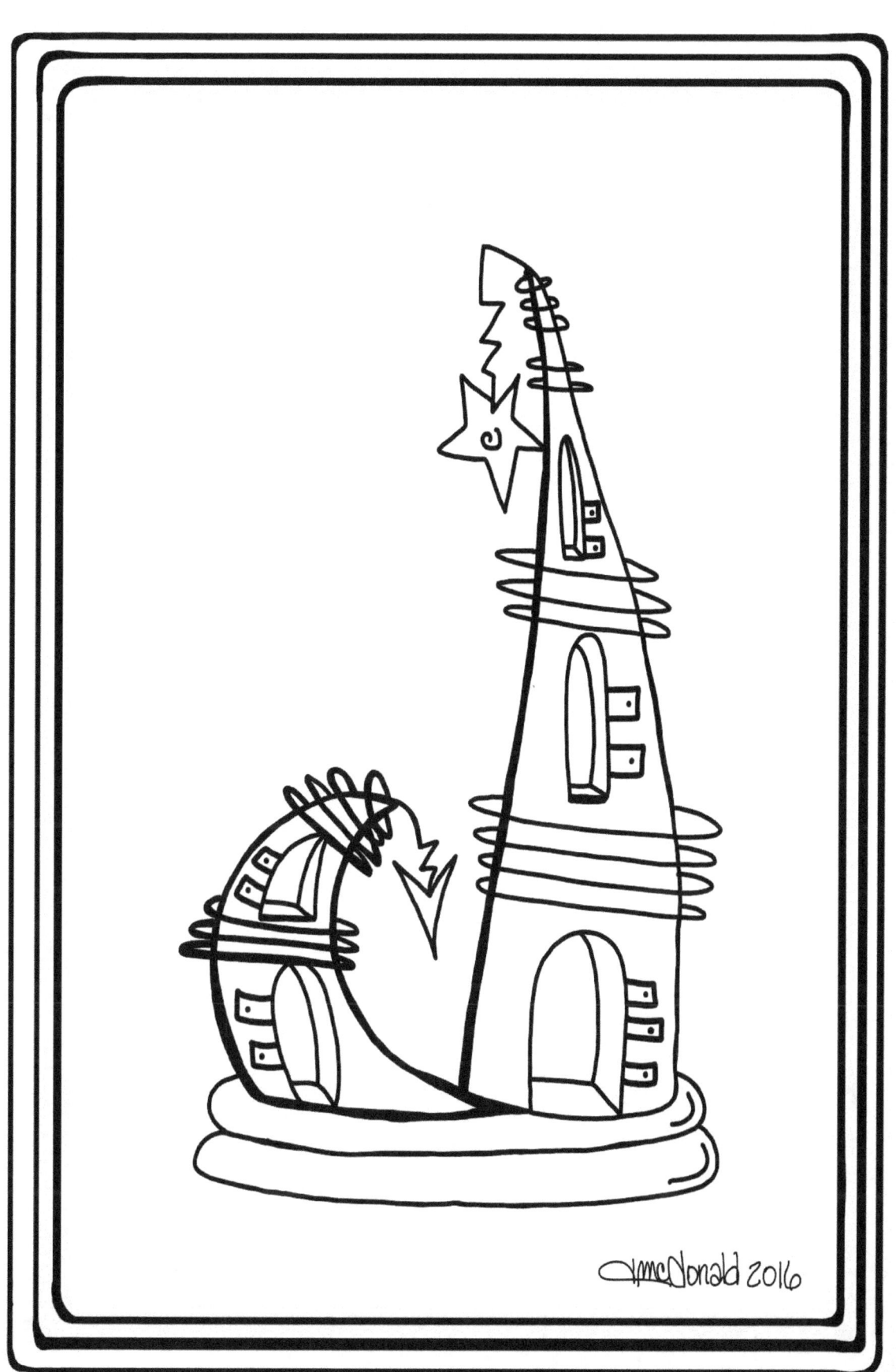

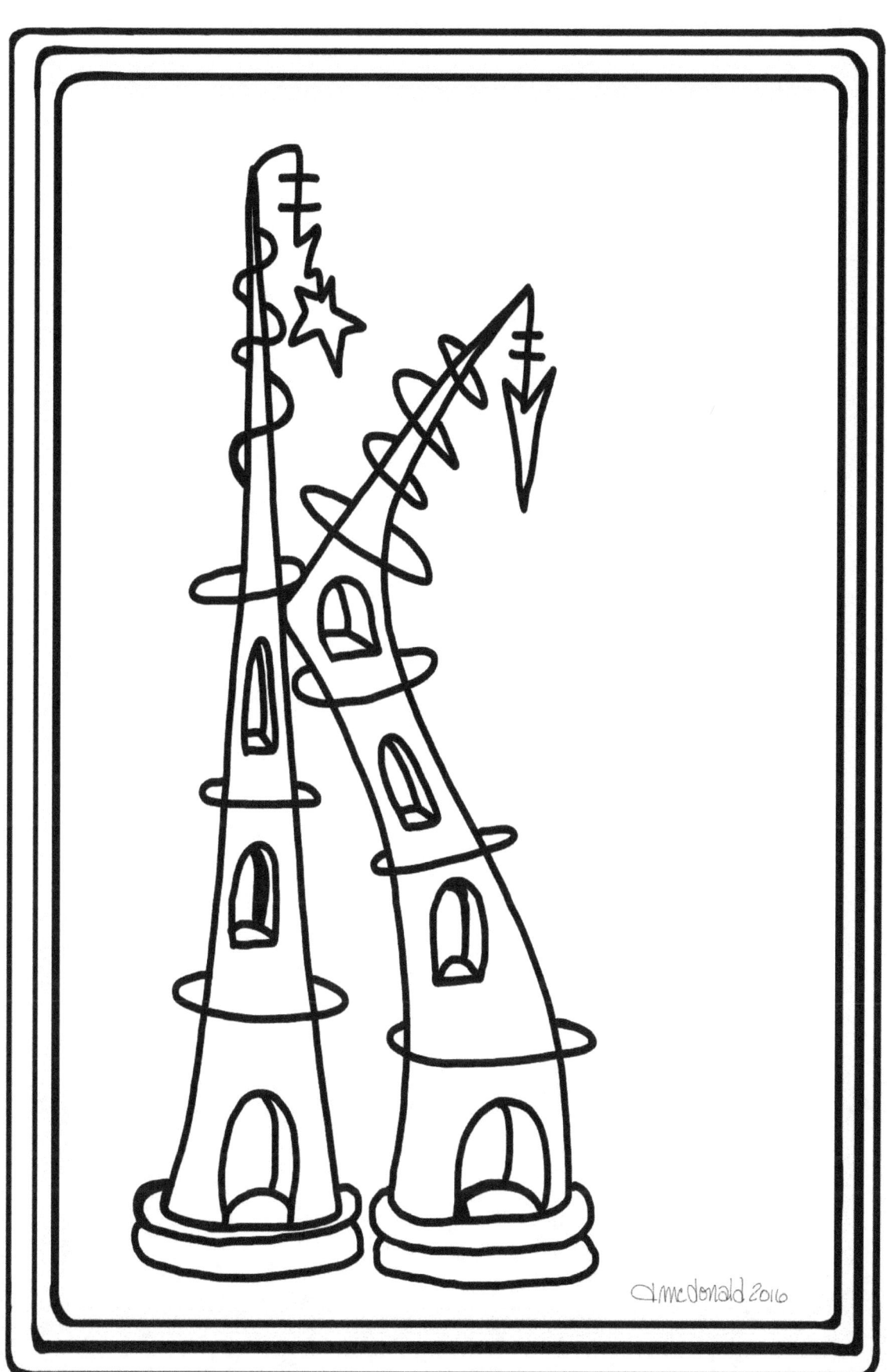

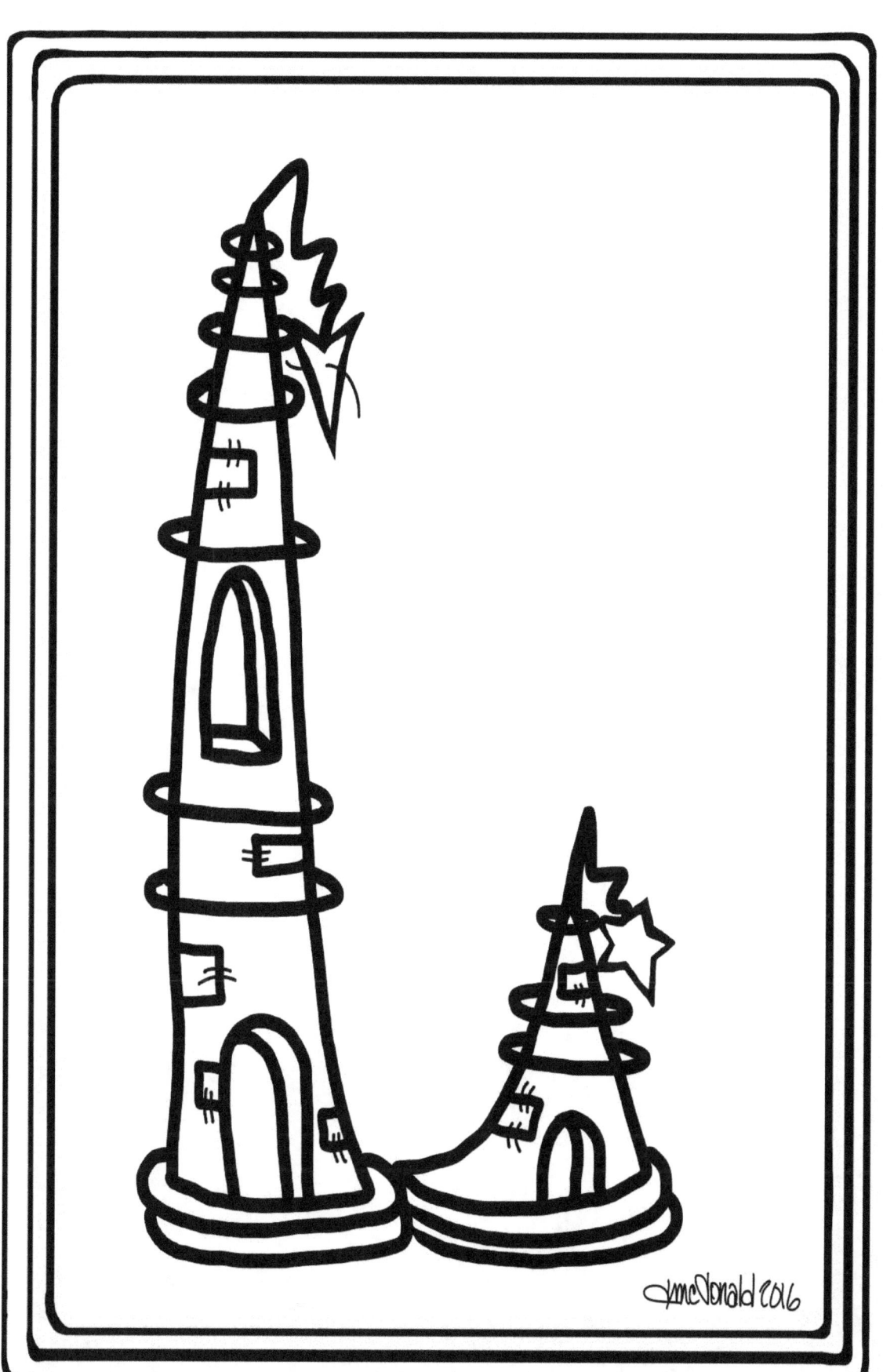

JMcDonald 2016

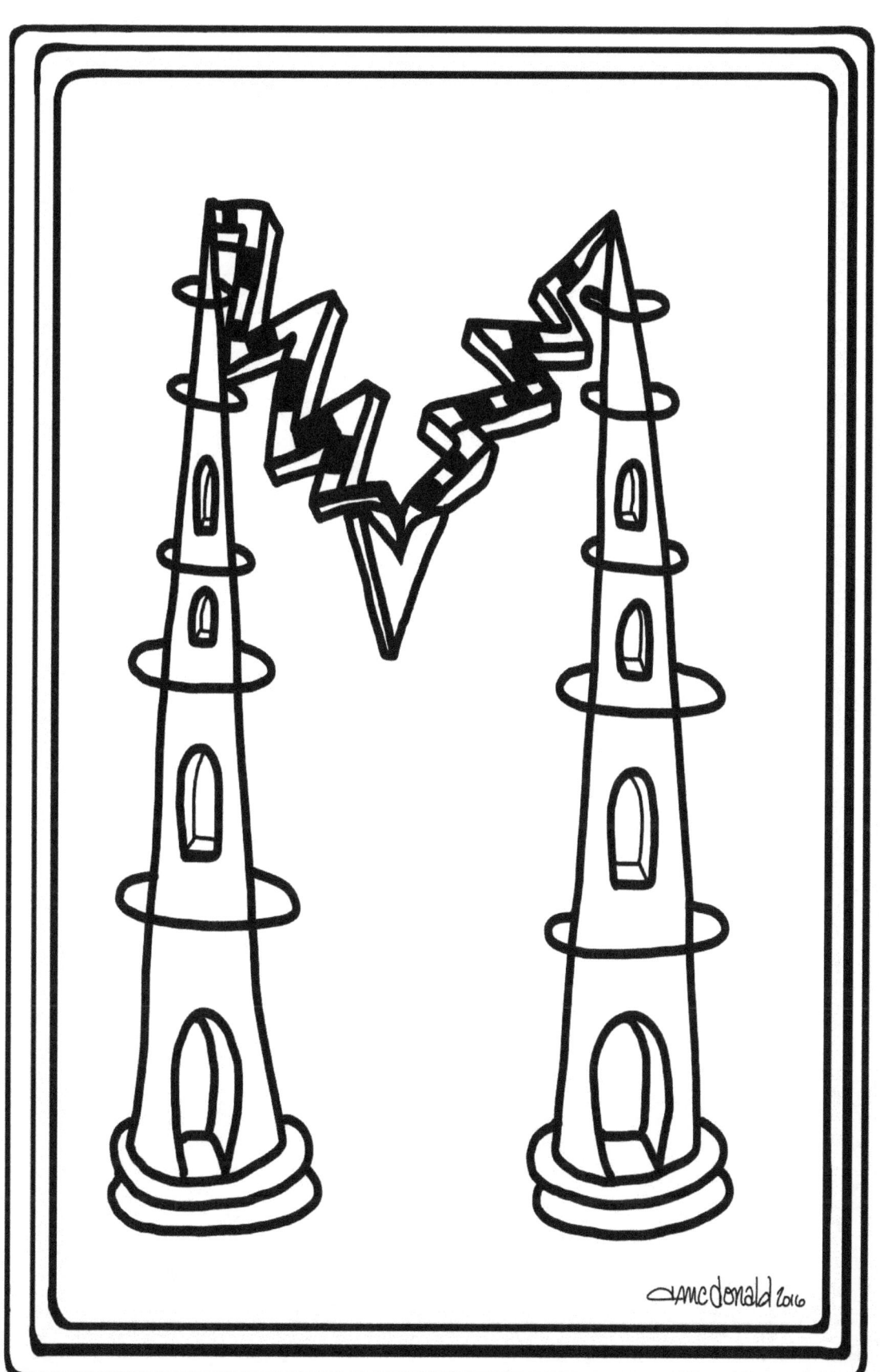

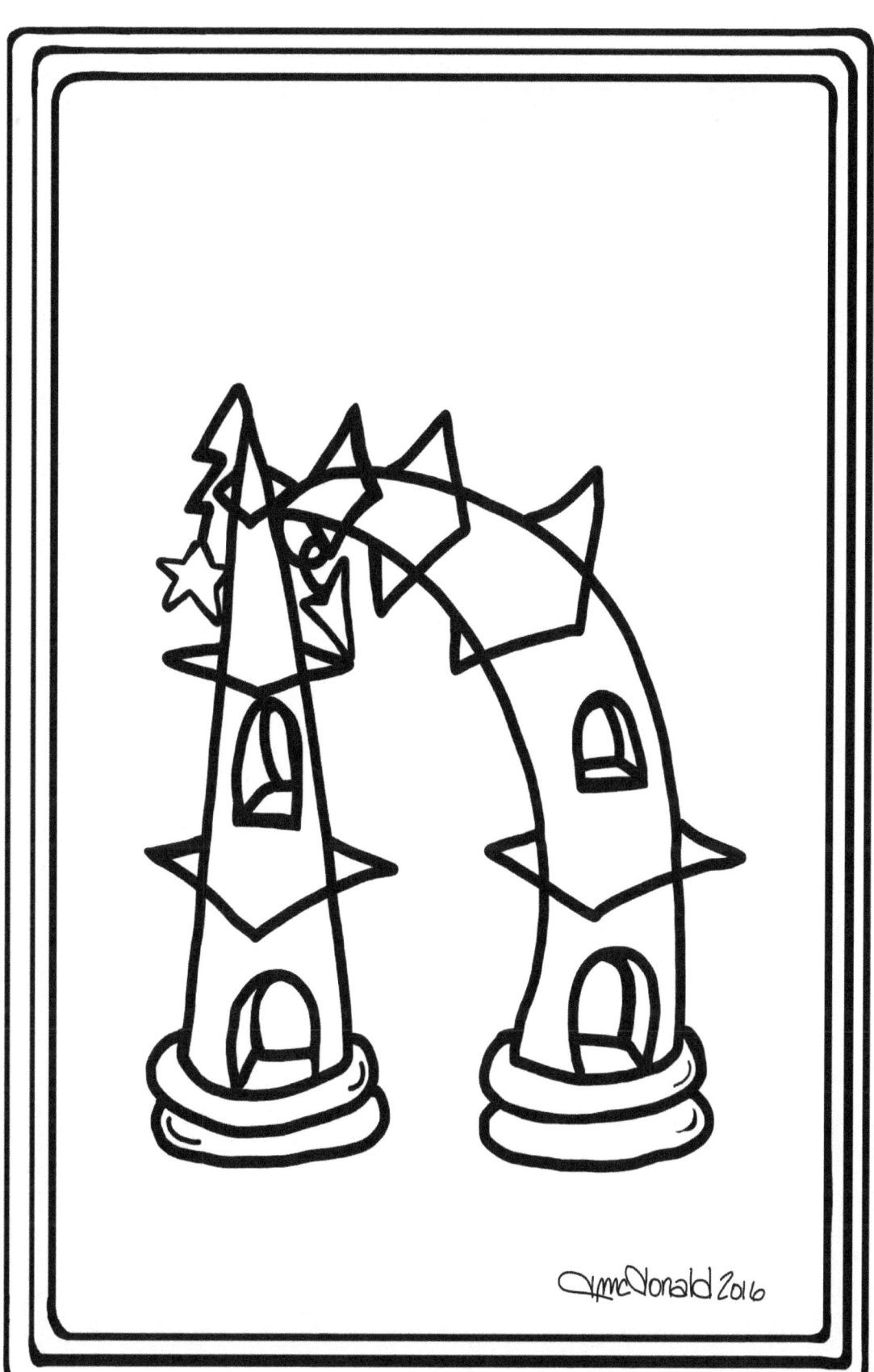

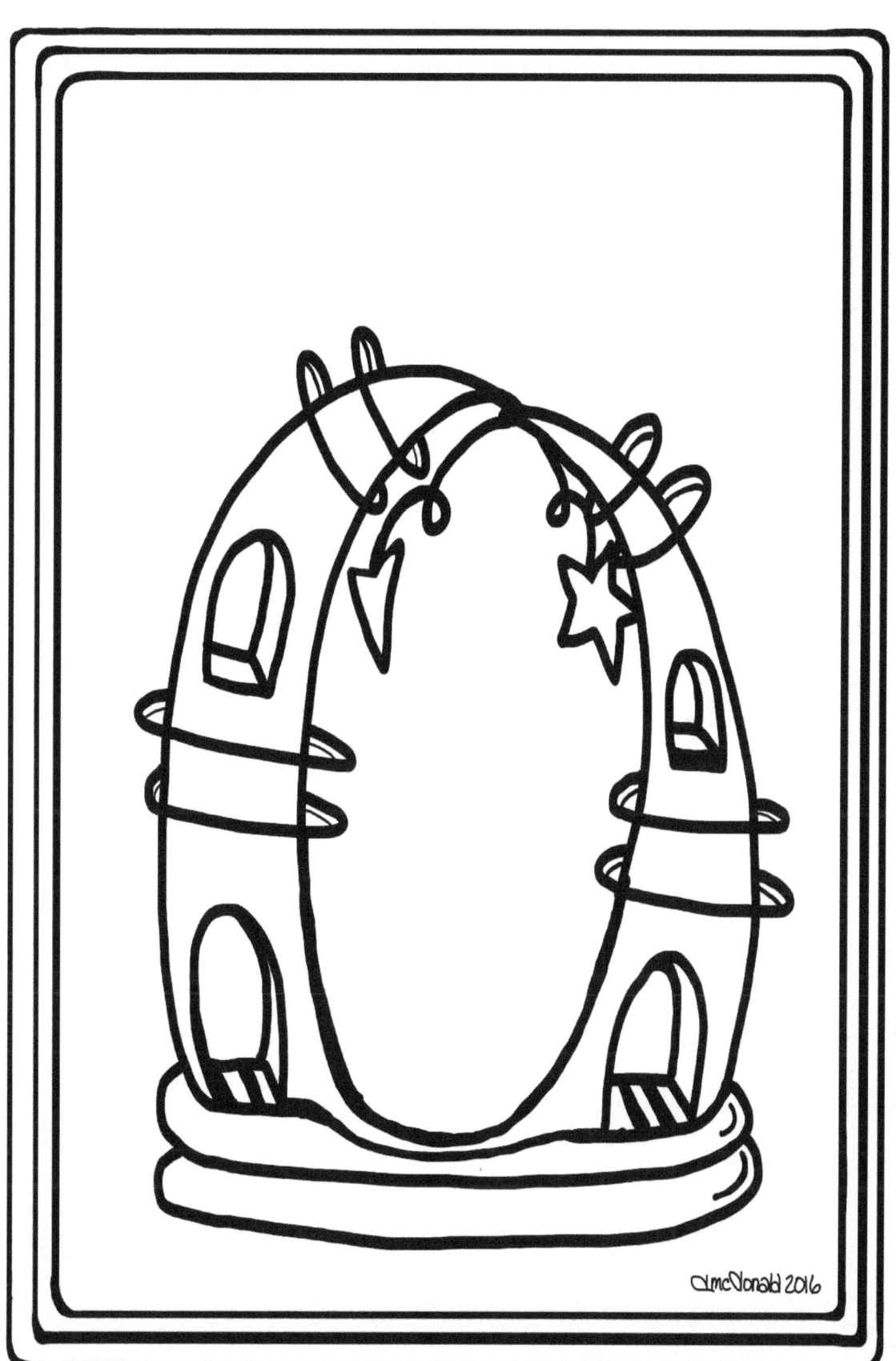

cmcDonald 2016

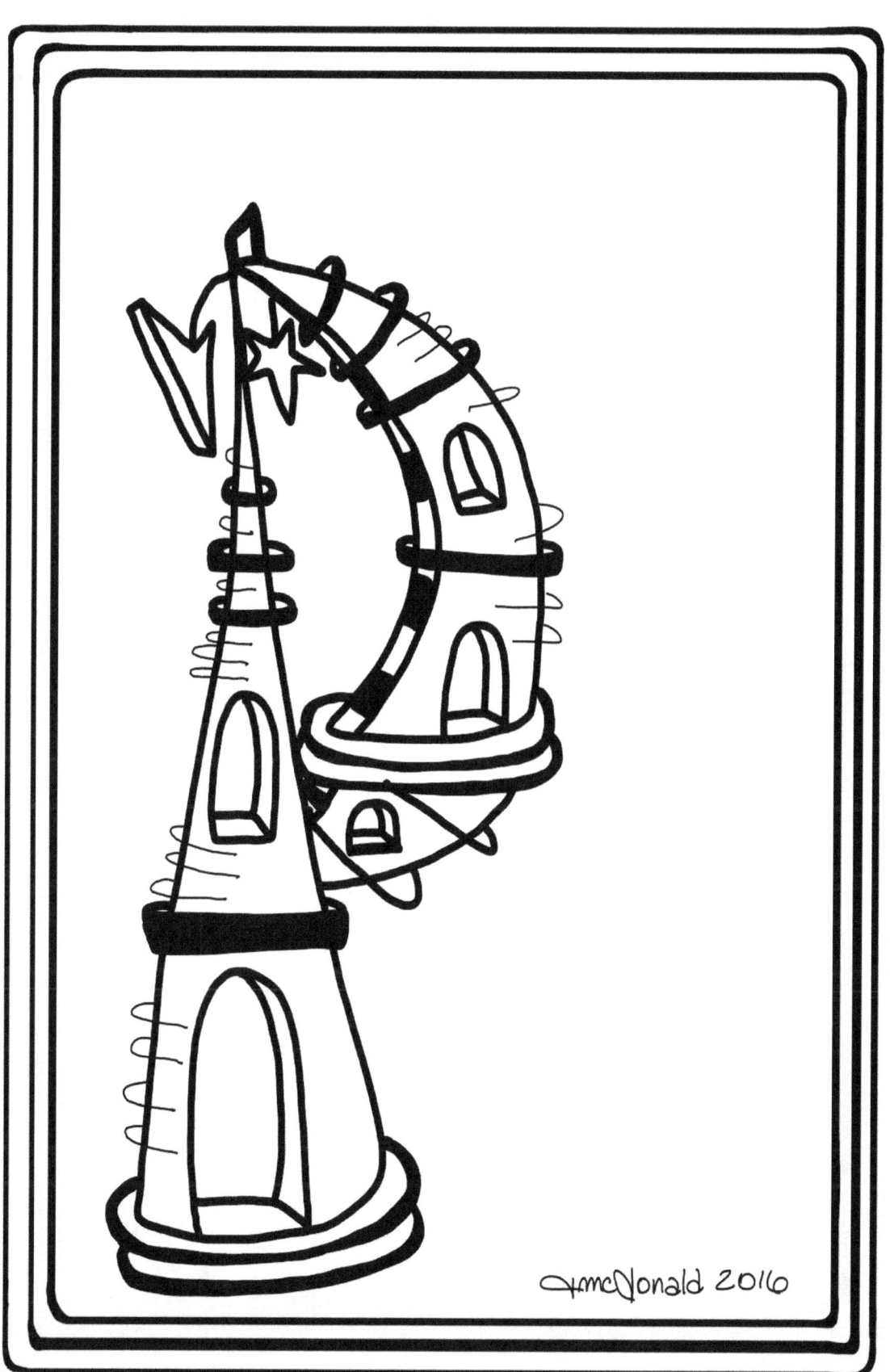

JmcDonald 2016

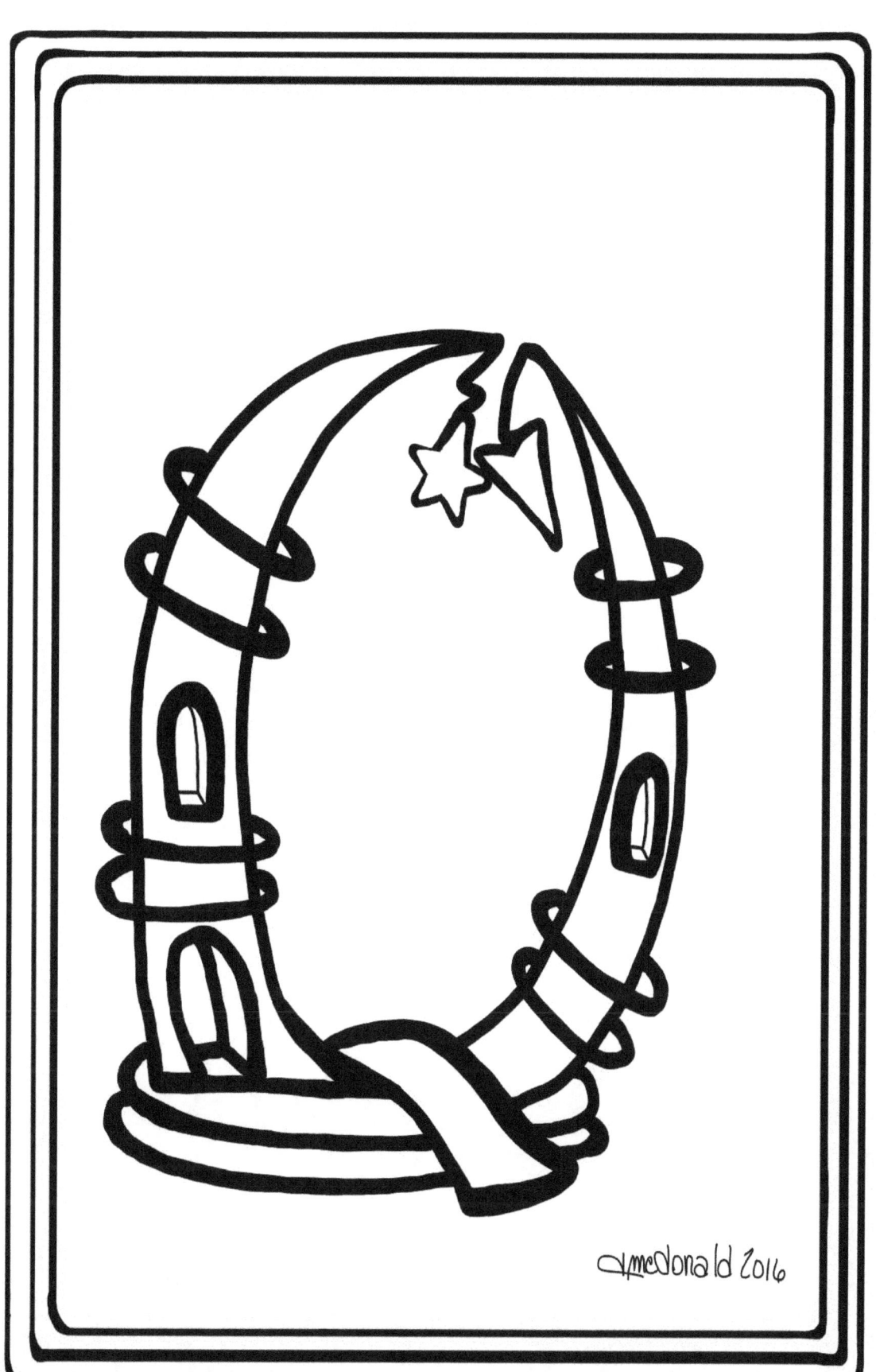

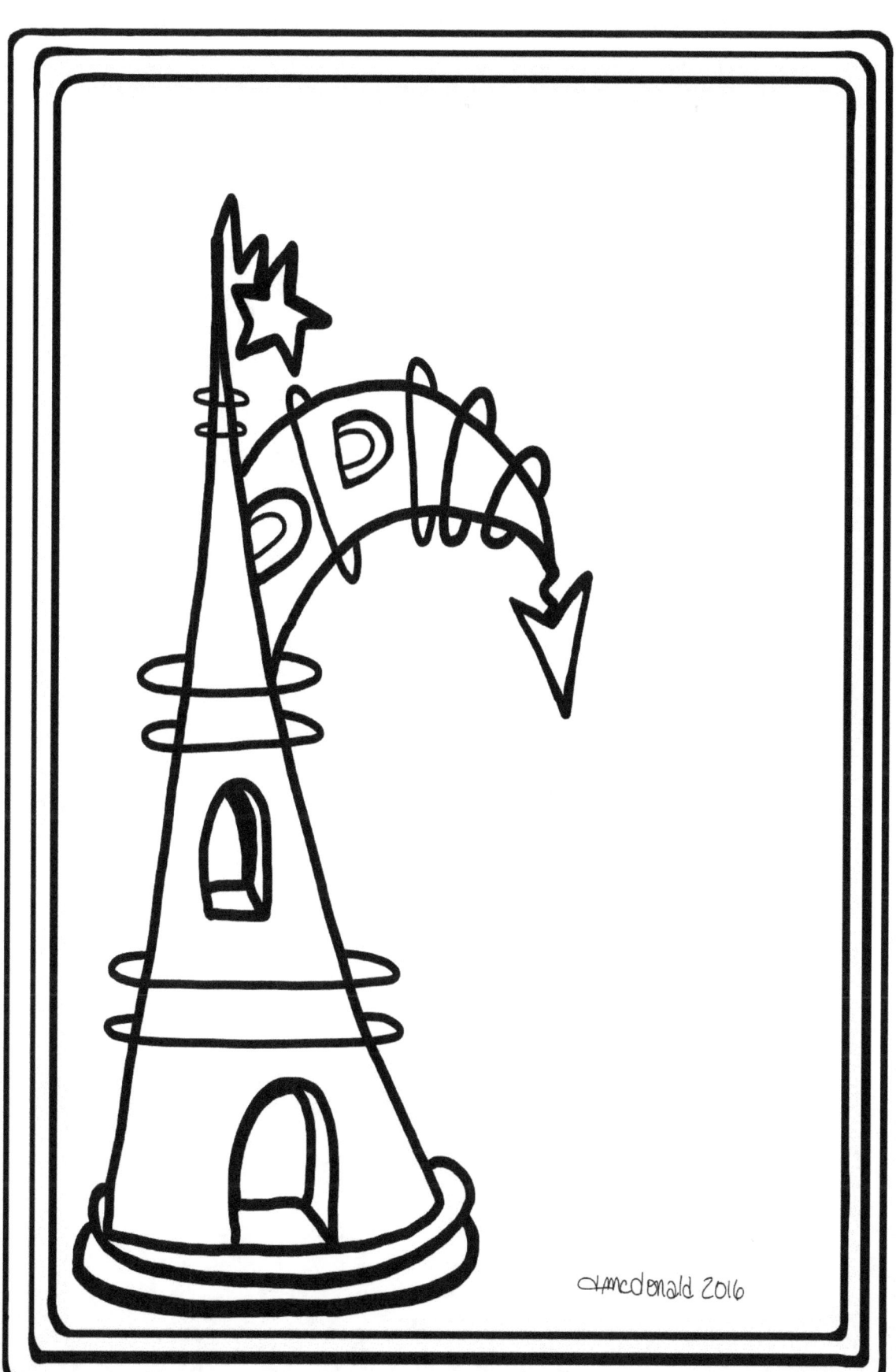

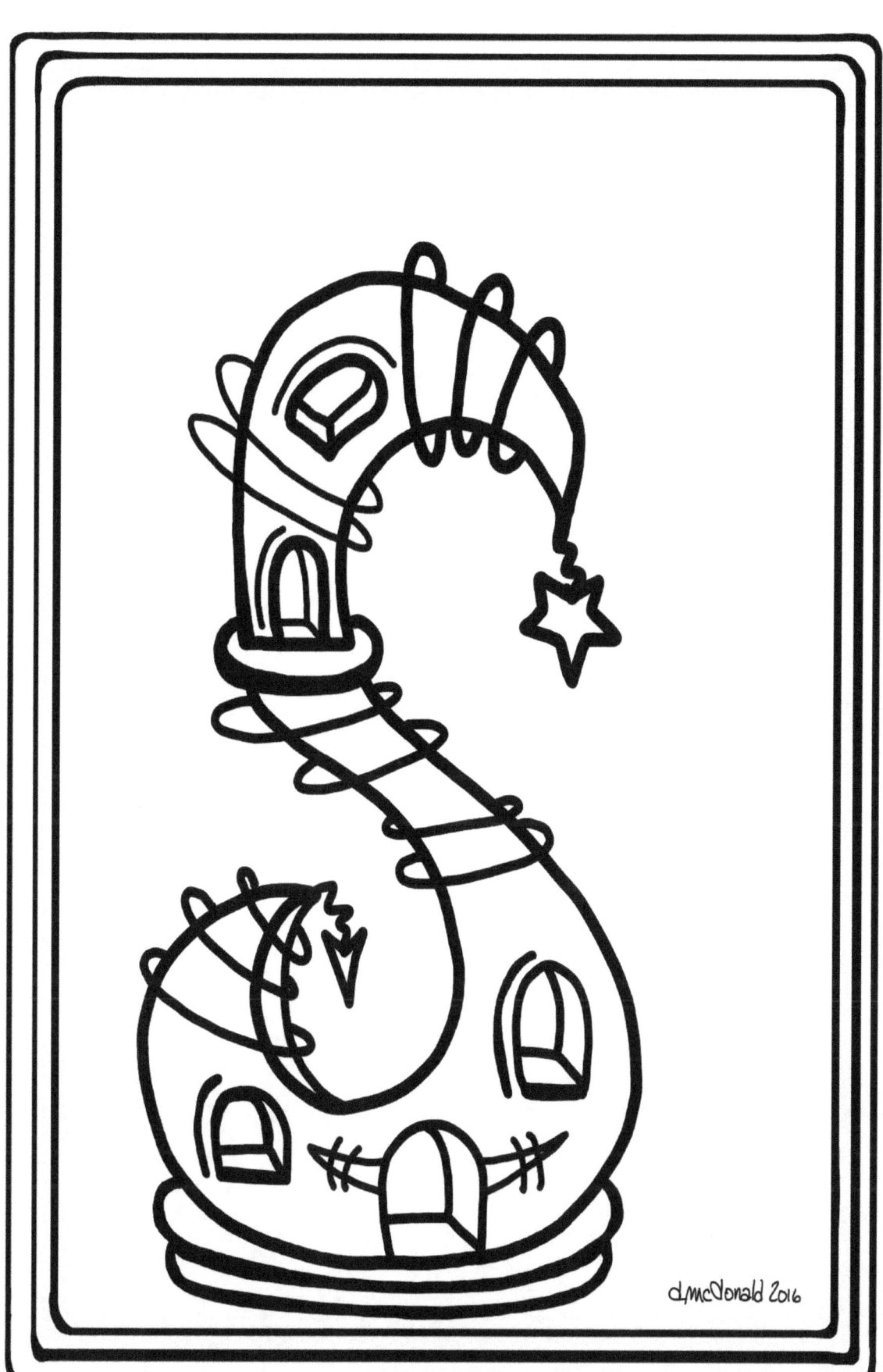

d.mcdonald 2016

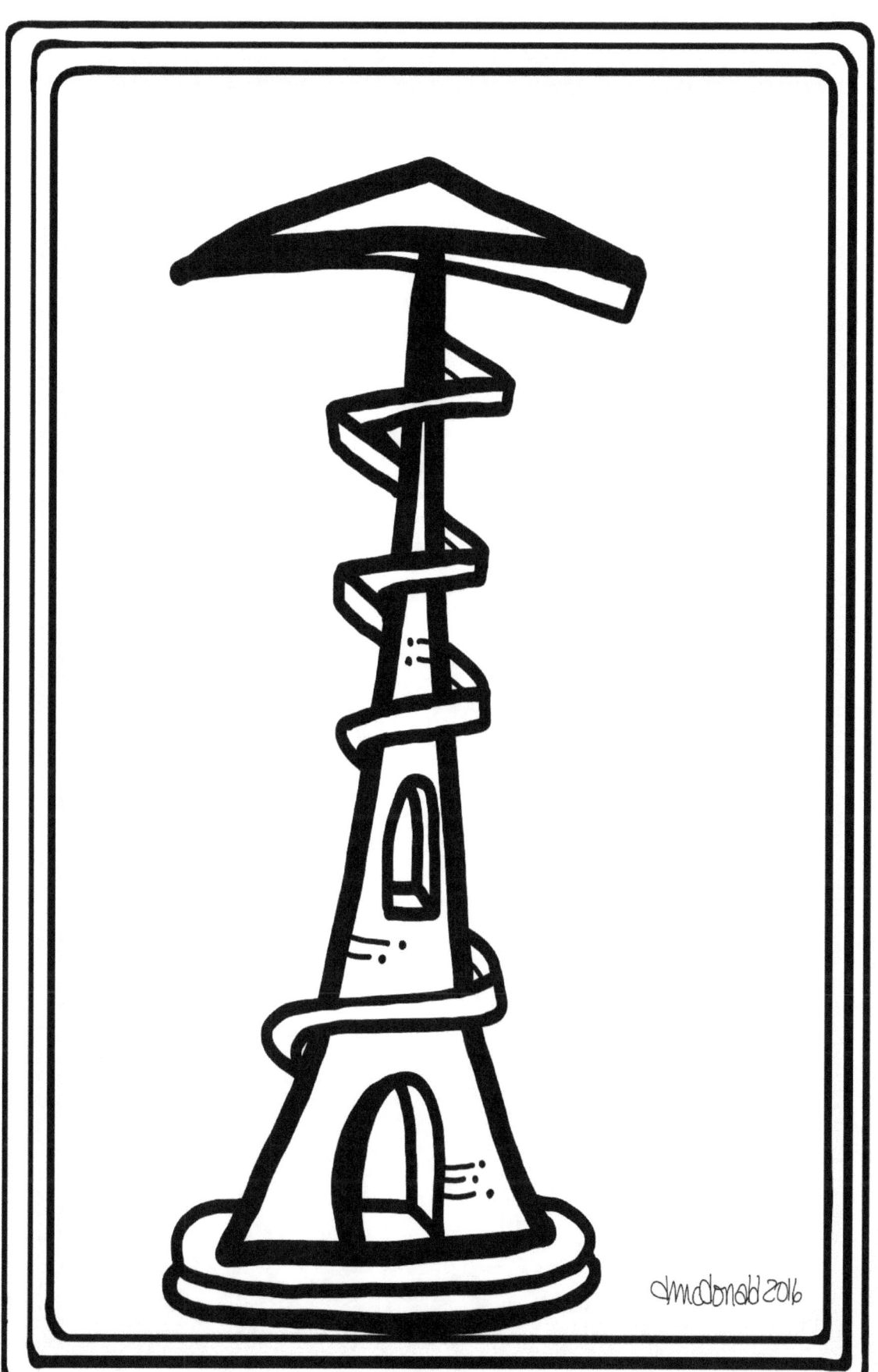

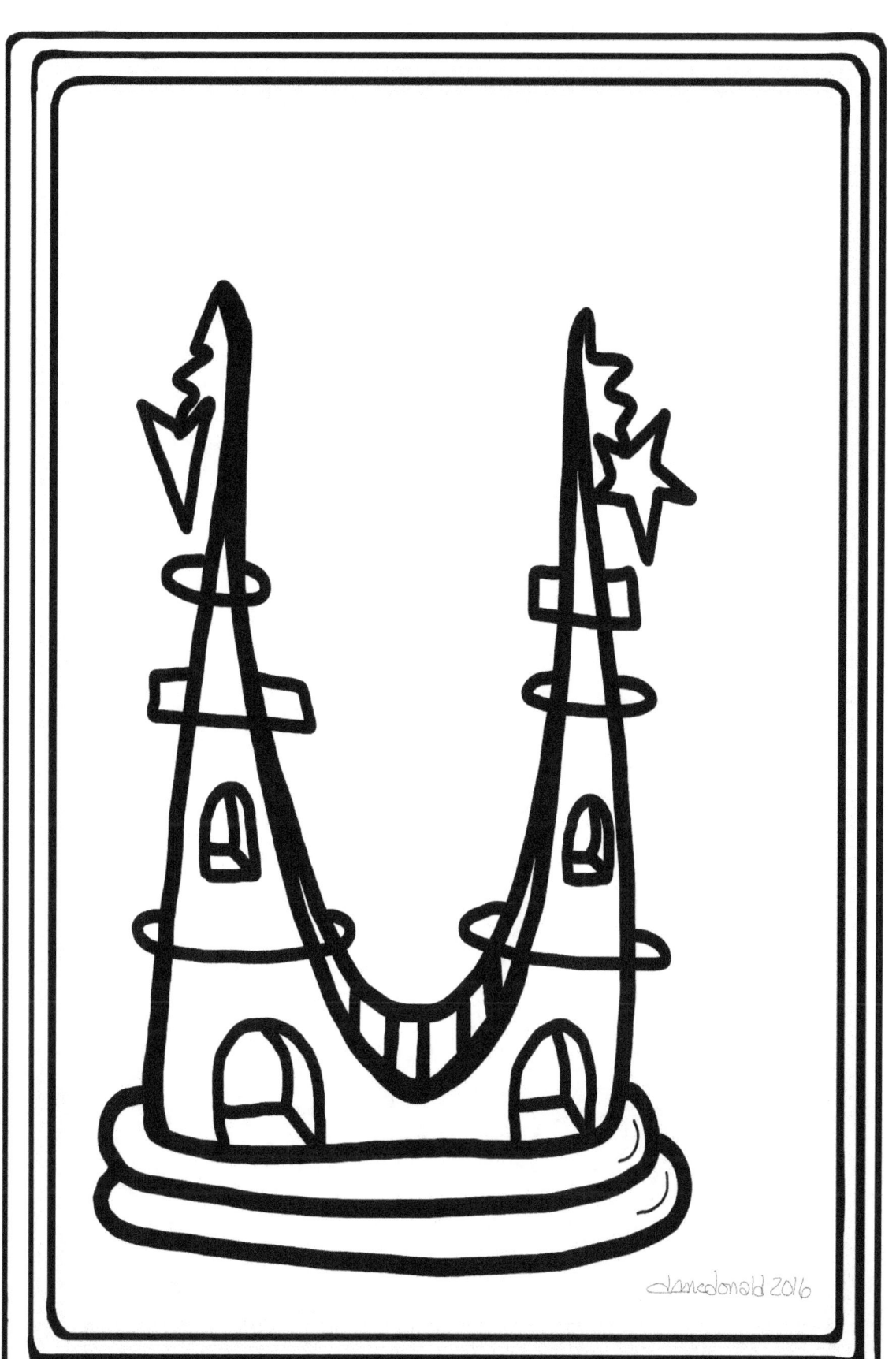

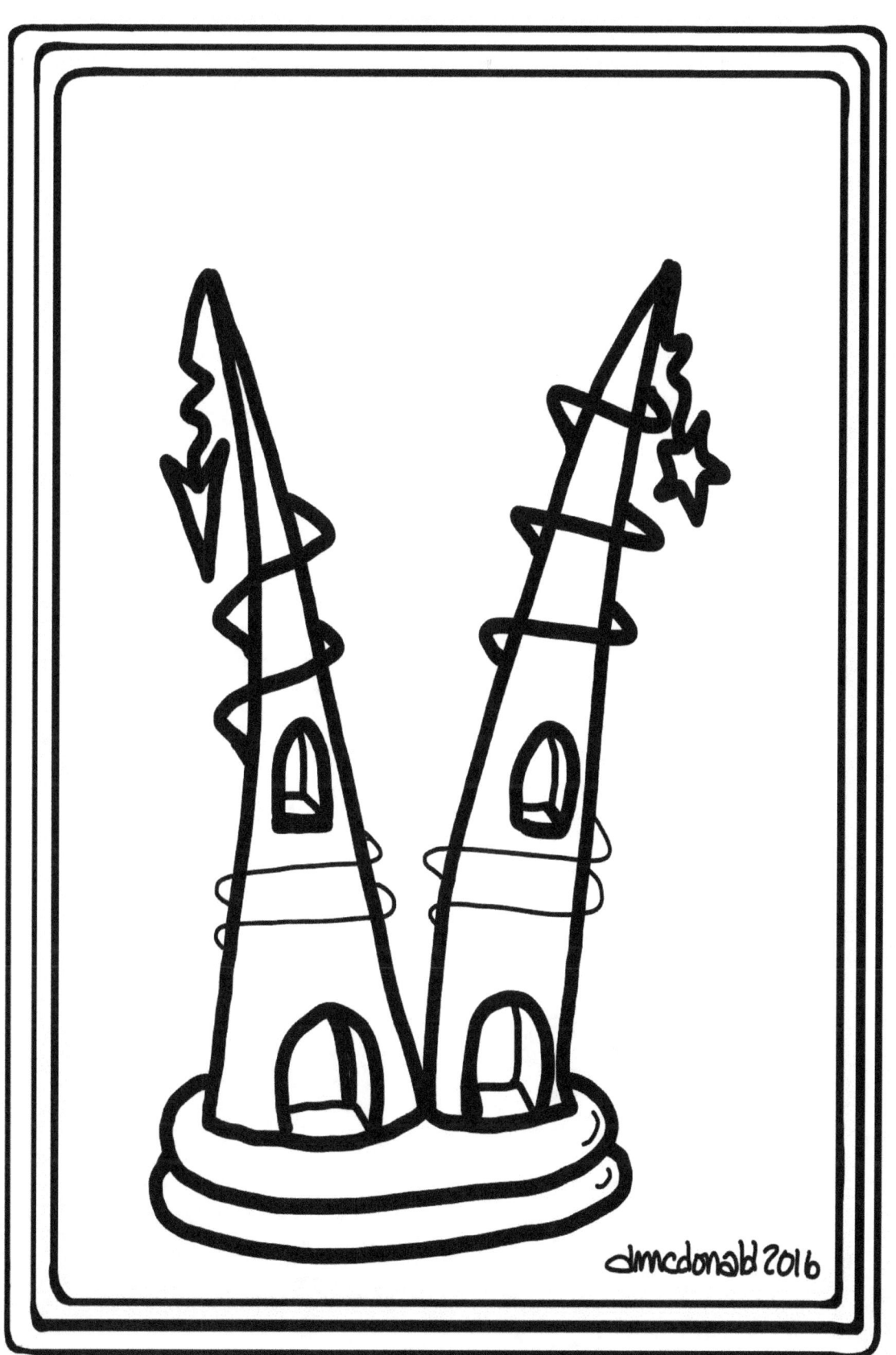

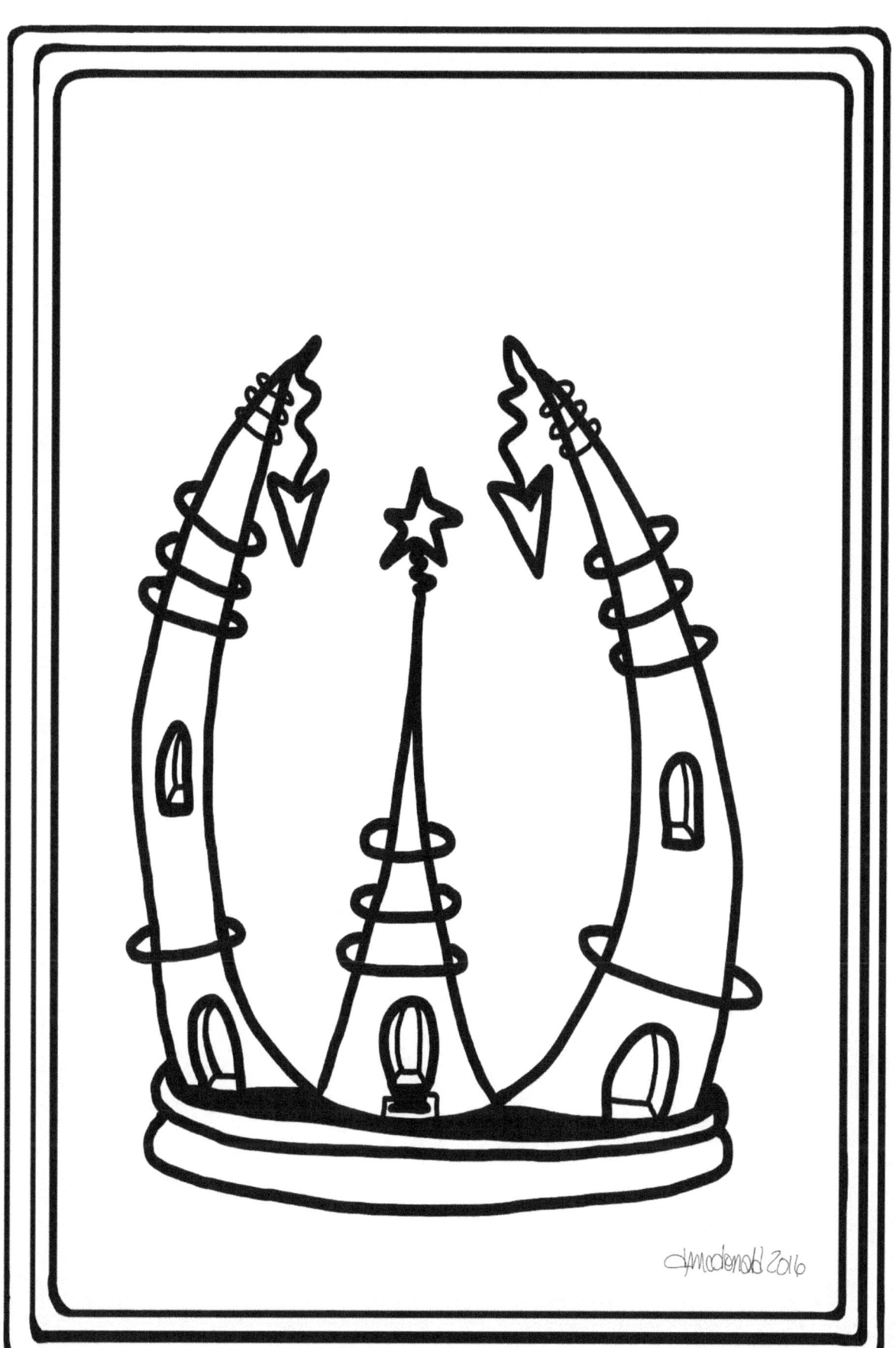

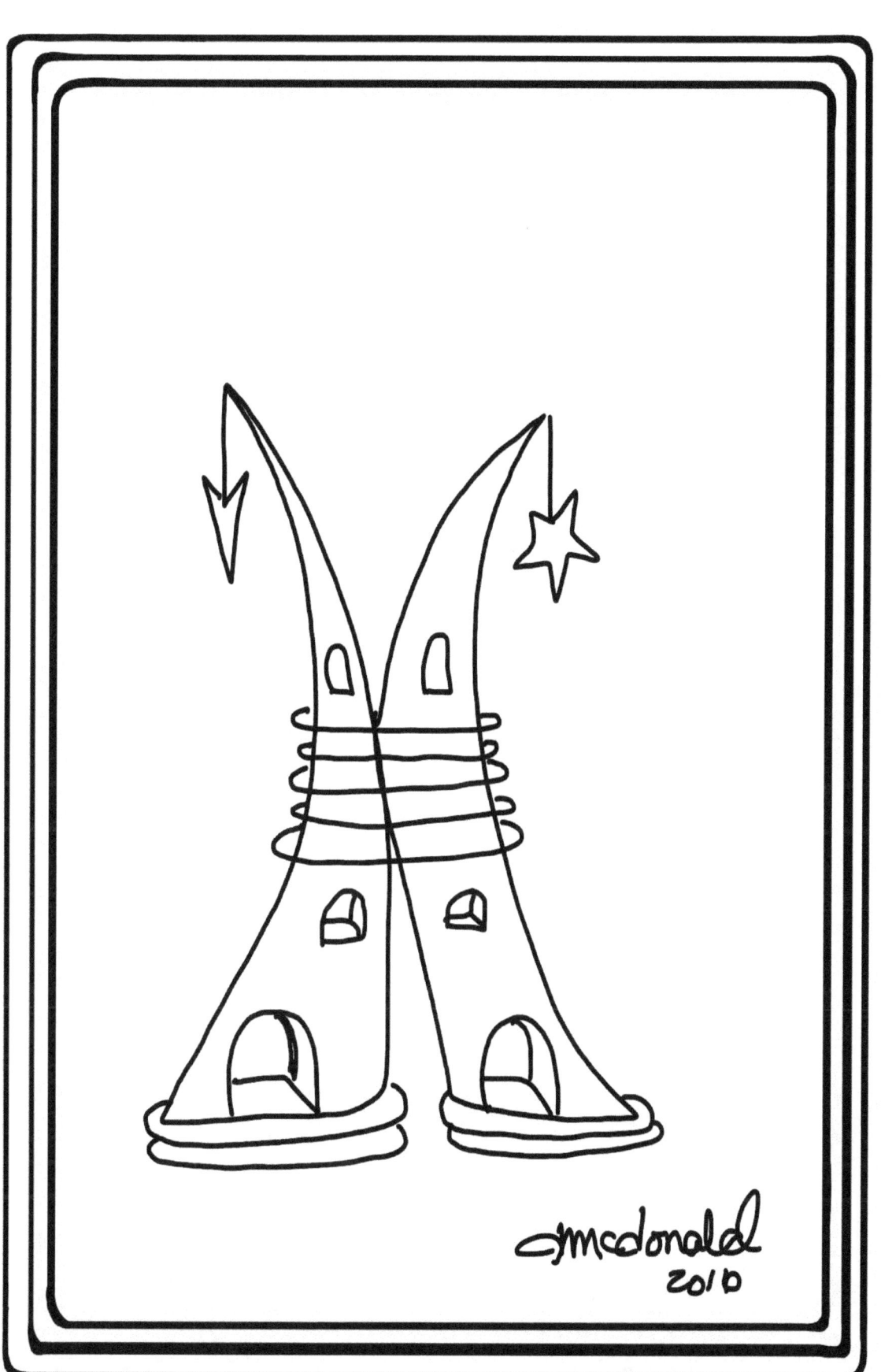

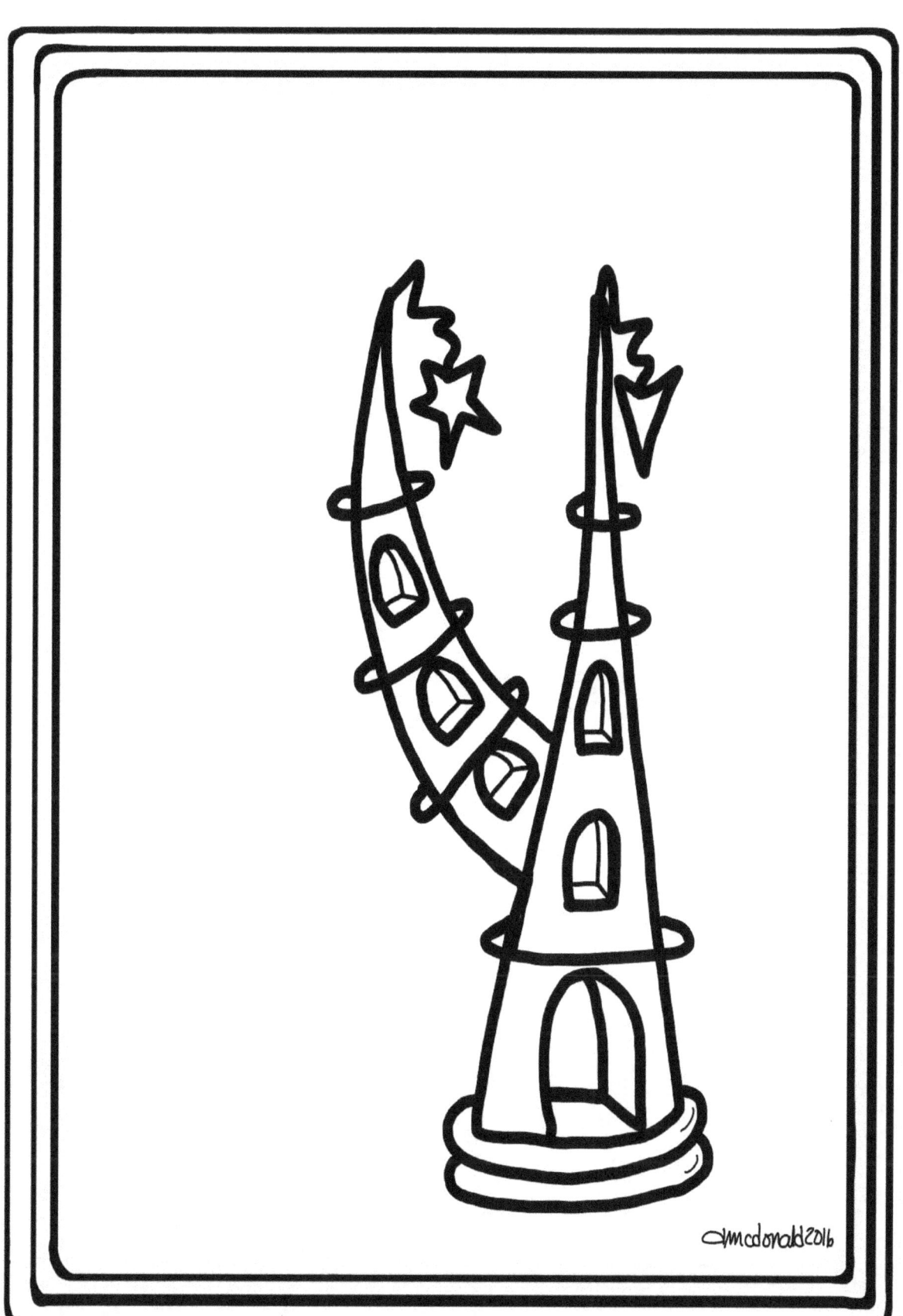

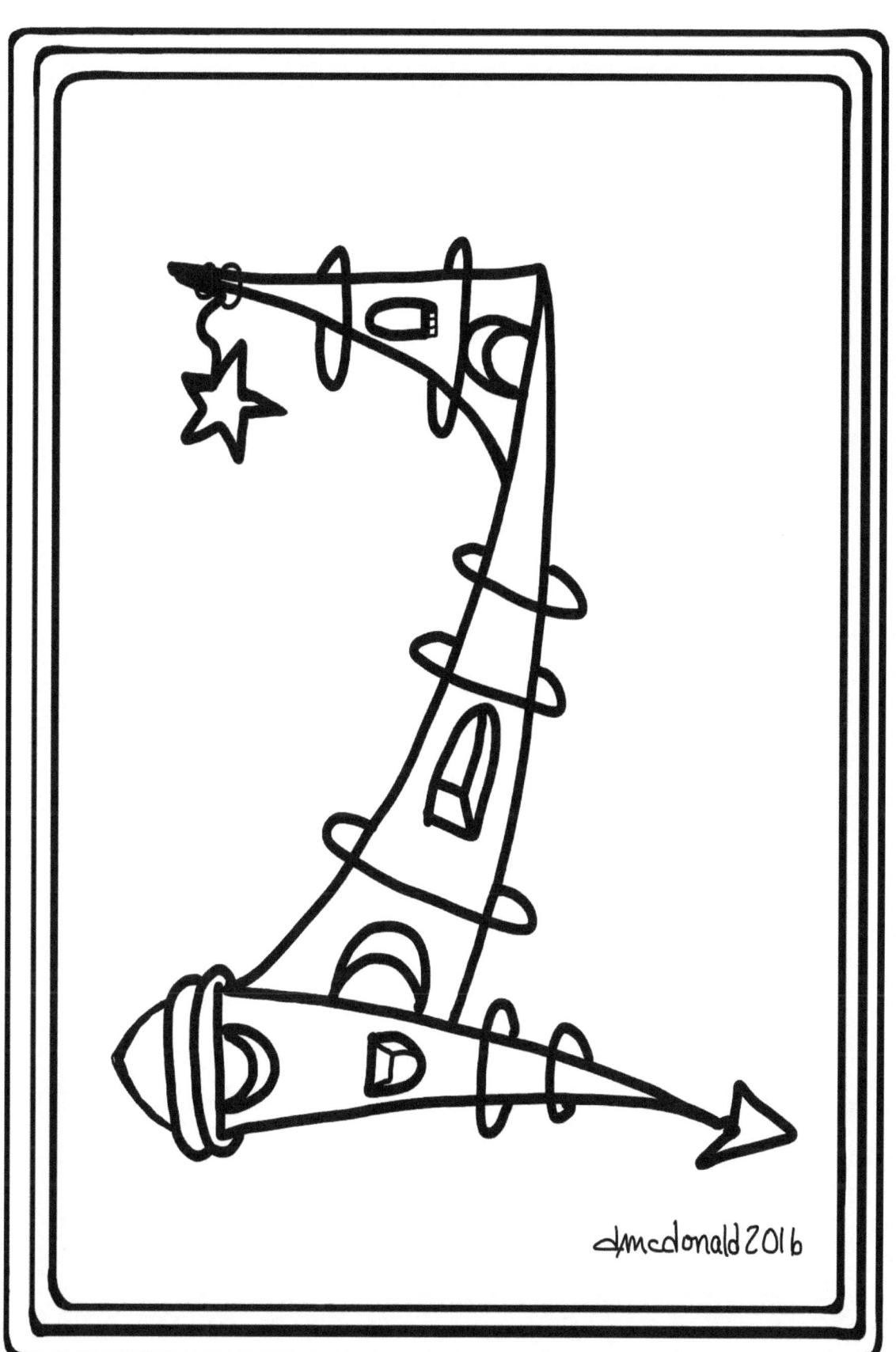

dmcdonald 2016

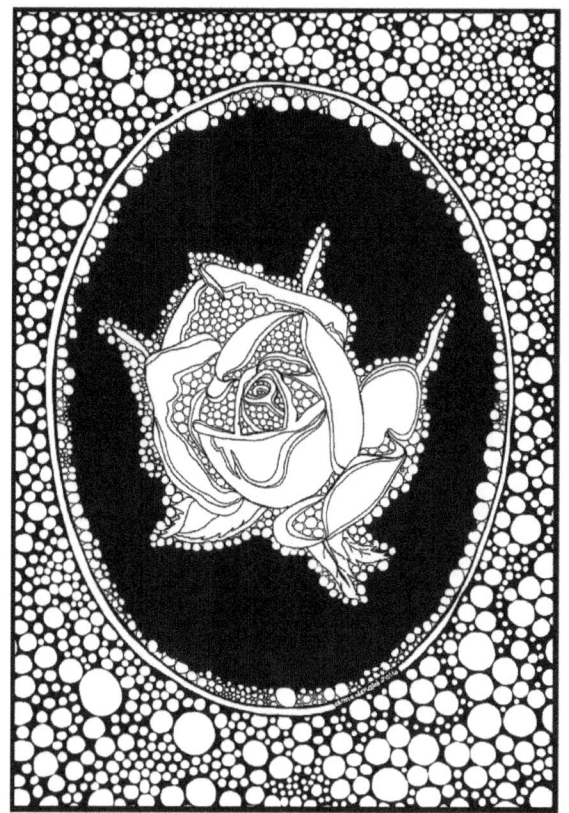
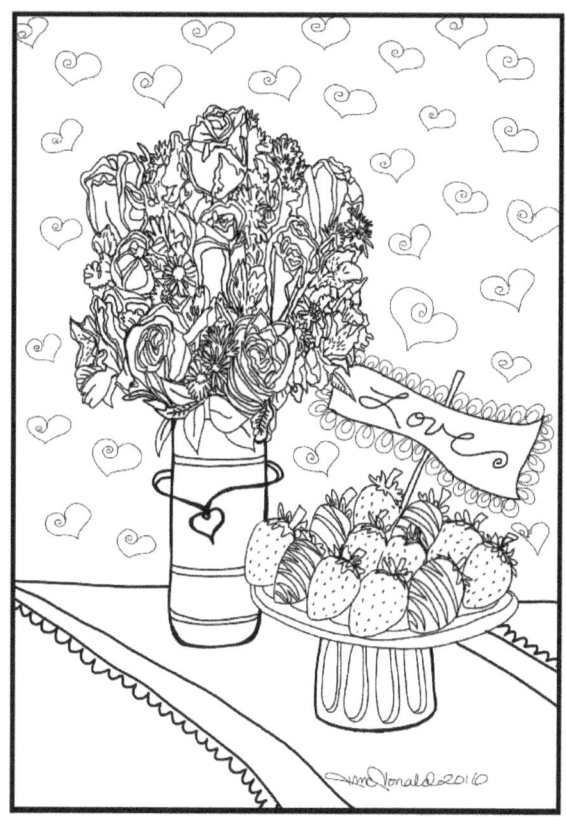

SAMPLES From: d.McDonald Designs Floral Adult Coloring Book Collection

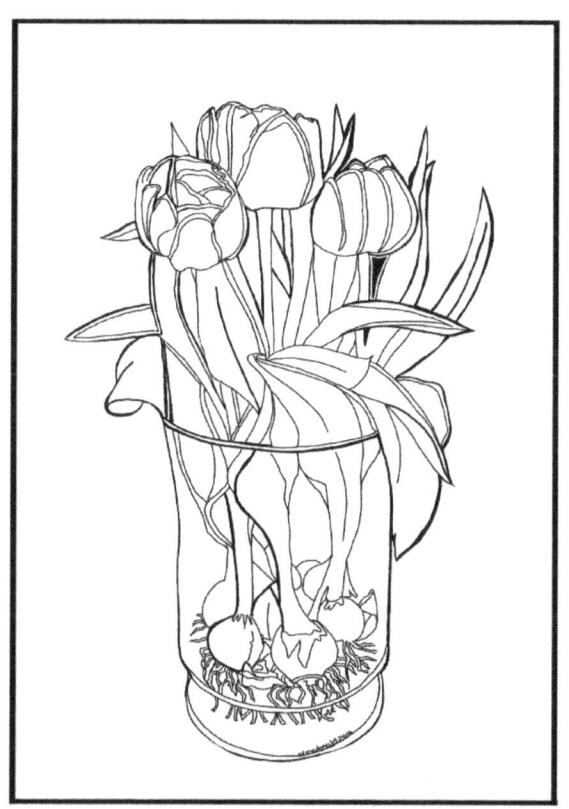
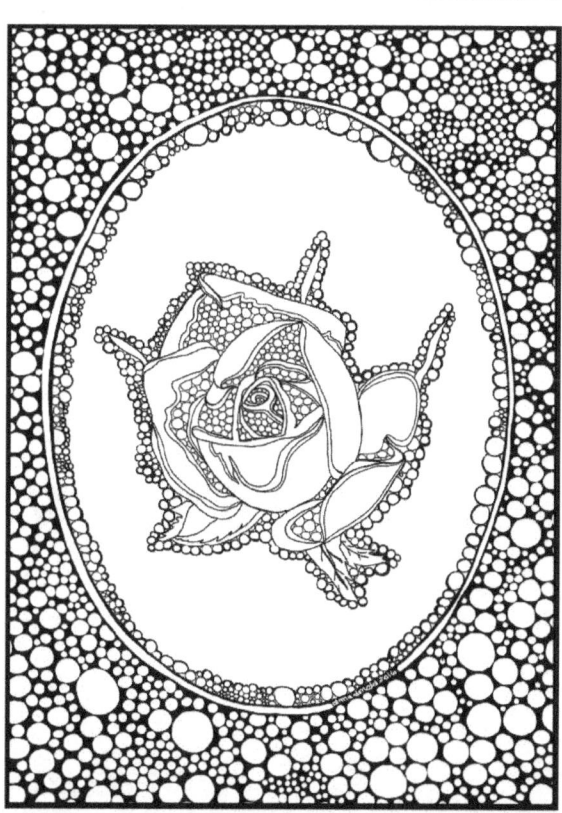

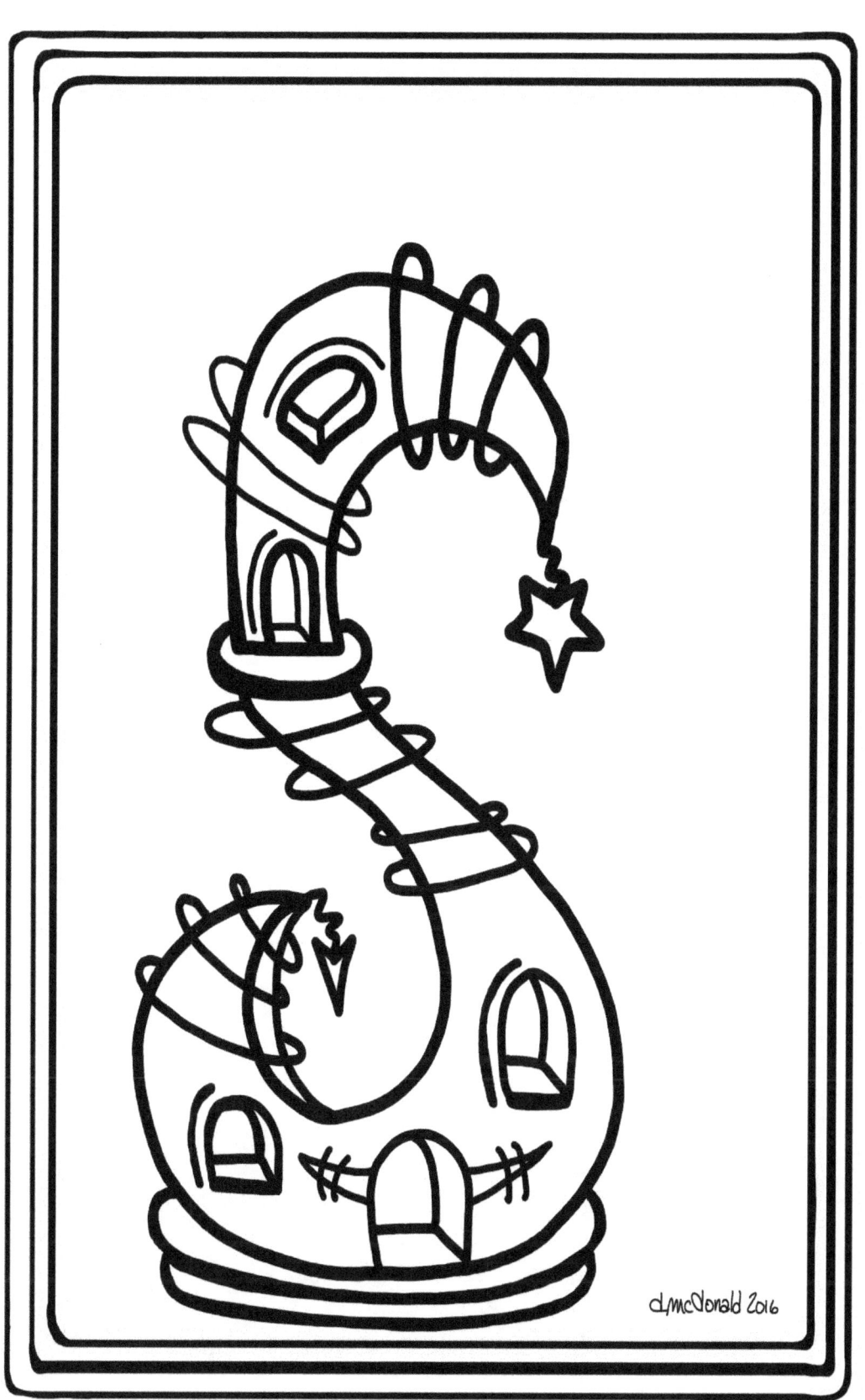

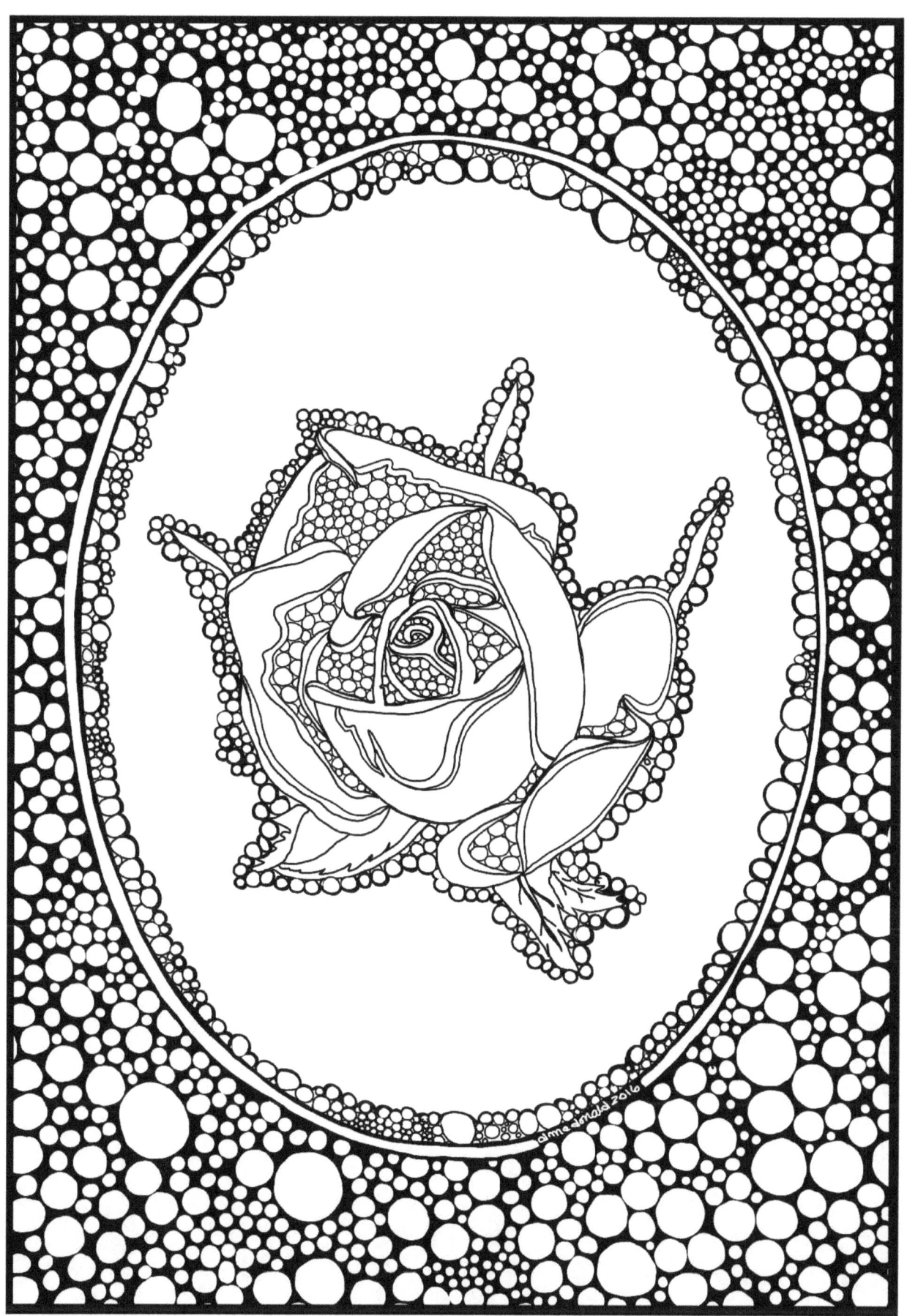

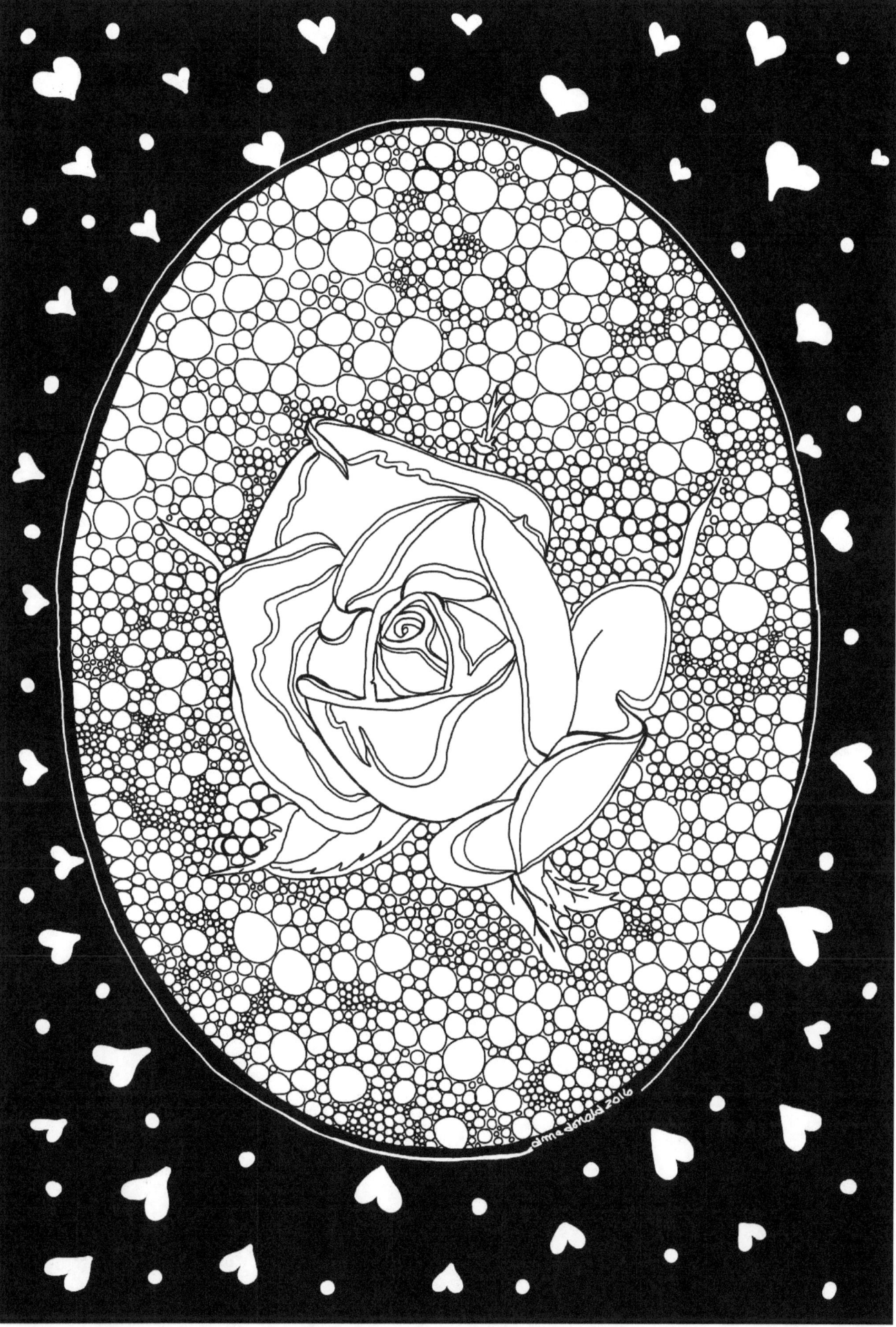

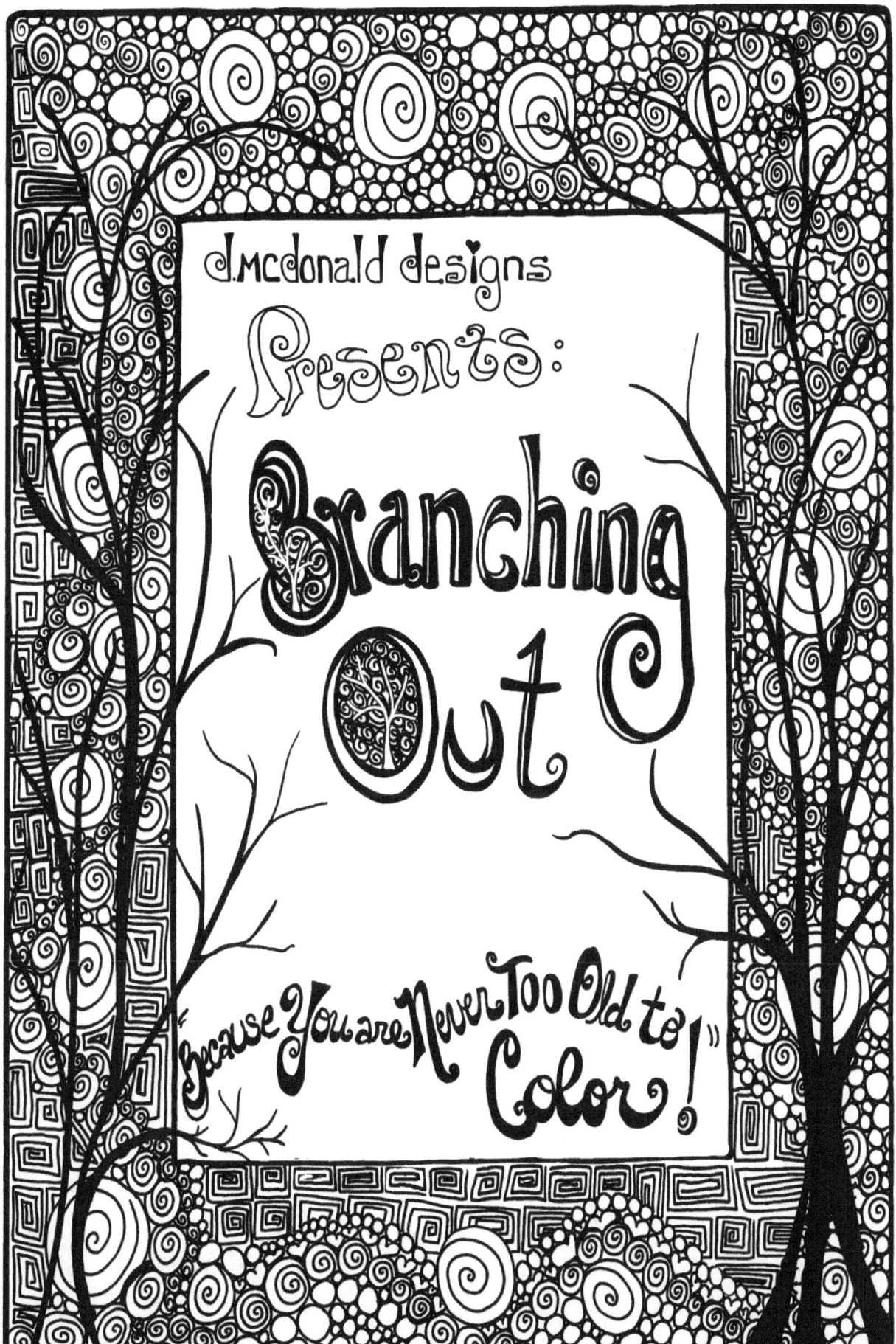

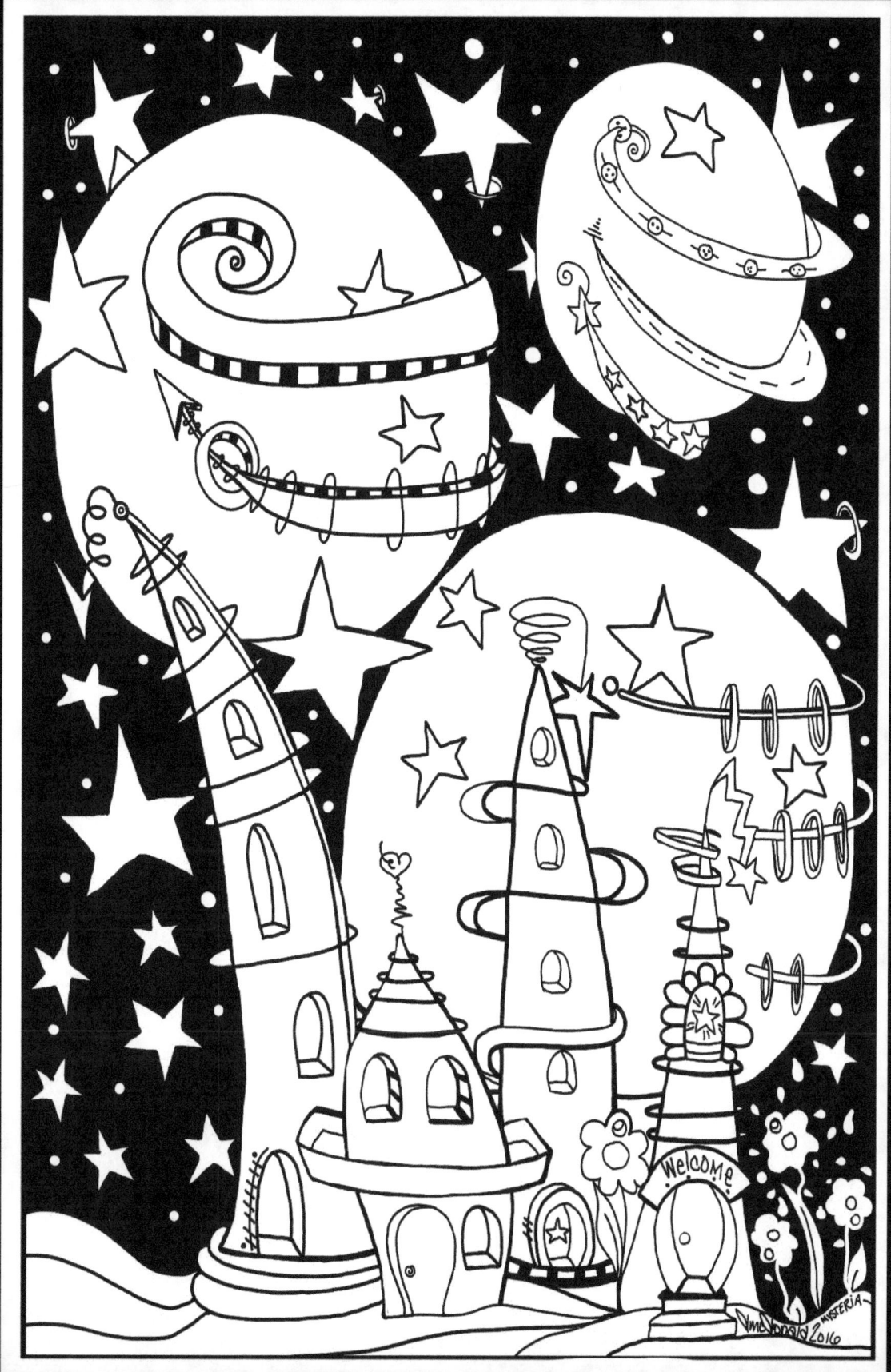

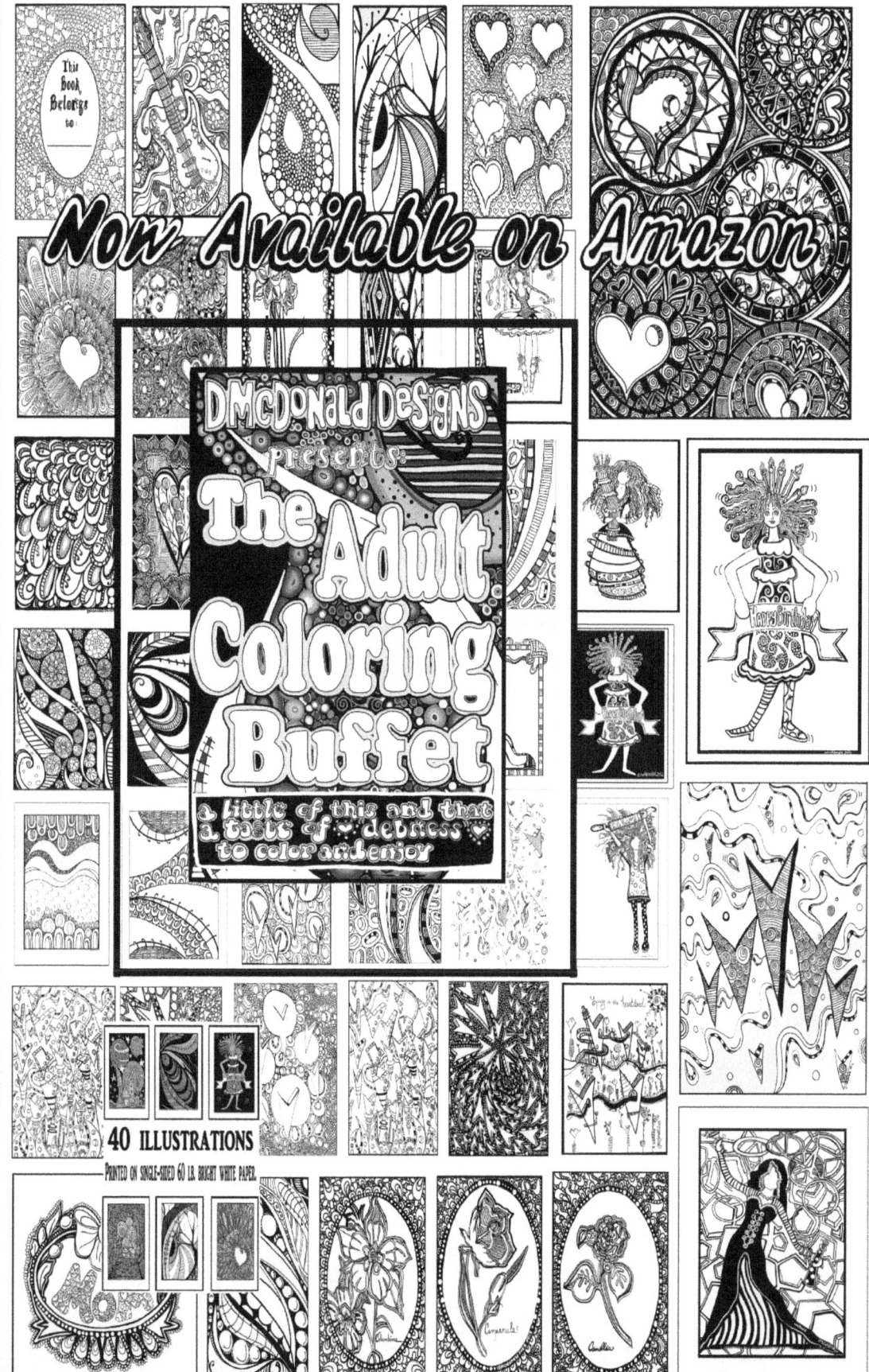

Now Available on Amazon

This Book Belongs to:

DMcDonald Designs
presents
The Adult Coloring Buffet
a little of this and that
a taste of ♥ deliciousness ♥
to color and enjoy

40 ILLUSTRATIONS
PRINTED ON SINGLE-SIDED 60 LB. BRIGHT WHITE PAPER

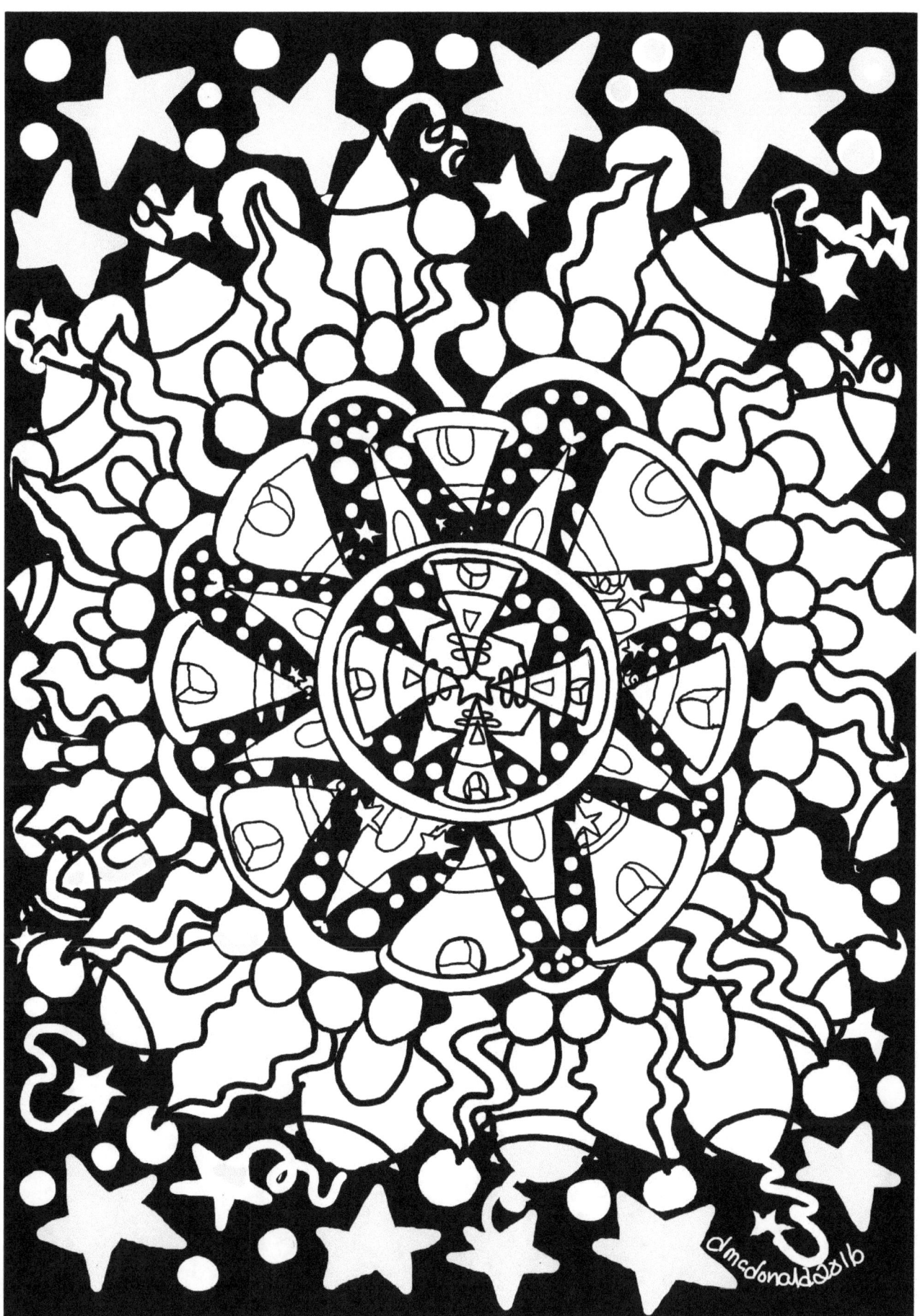

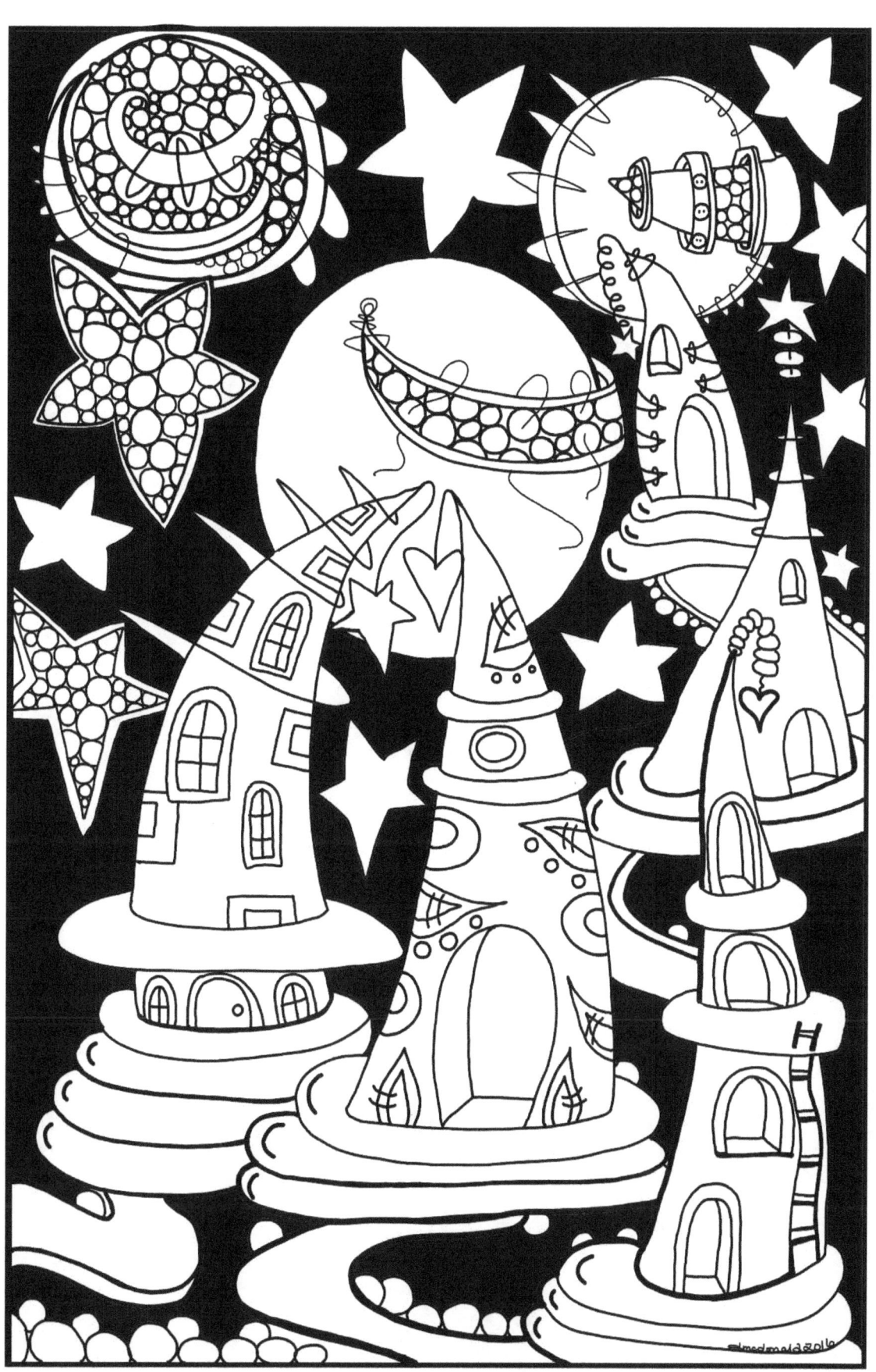

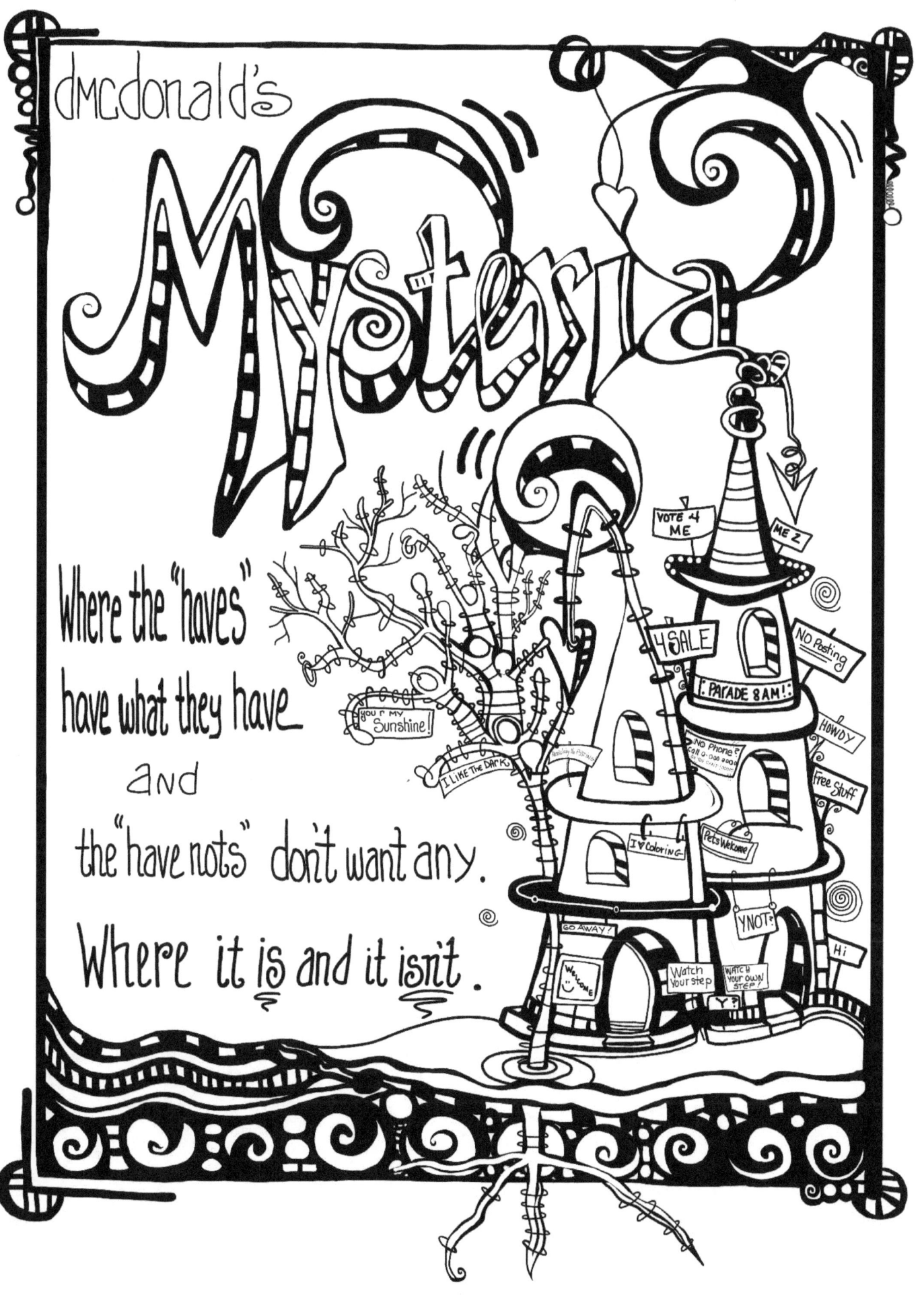

Hope
You
Had
Fun

Some extra letters appear
And duplicates to try twice!